Dedicated to John Elliker, who has the true Emily Dickinson spirit...

and

Patricia McCambridge, whose writing has shaped this book.
For her hours of labor, long and hard, under the aegis of a fool,
my thanks, dear friend.

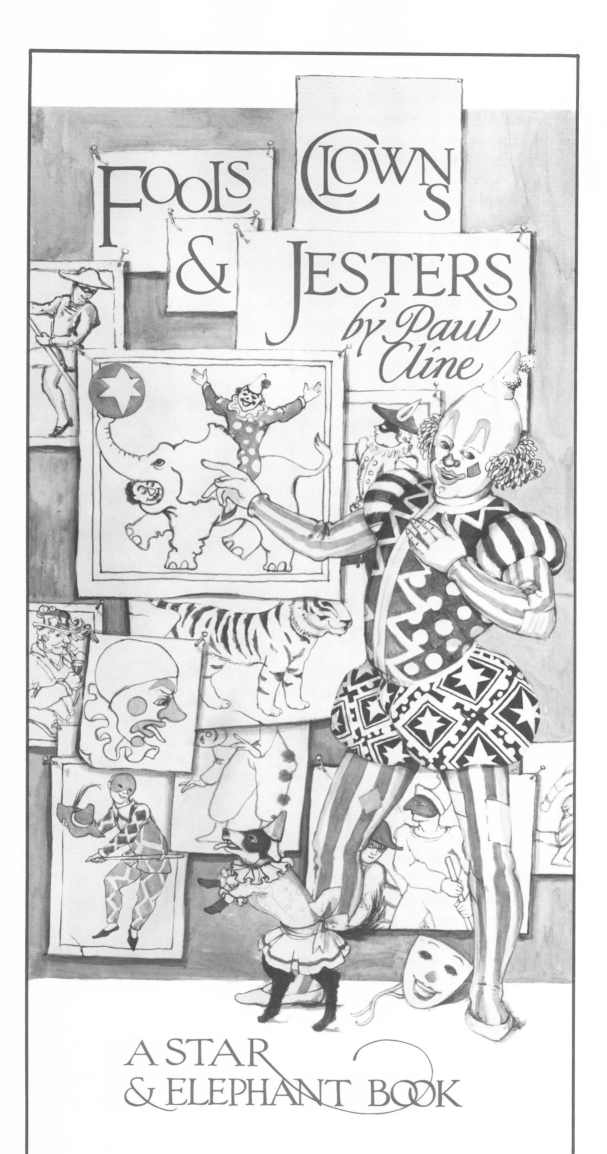

FOOLS CLOWNS & JESTERS

by Paul Cline

A STAR
& ELEPHANT BOOK

To Diana, Arie, Doff, Irina, Moyra, Sandy and John, Marie G., Angelina, Ron, Susan H., Peter and Shirley, John-John, Sandra and Harold and all the wonderful people at Green Tiger, especially to Patricia Mc. My thanks for their help, understanding, and, above all, friendship.

We are grateful to the following authors and publishers for the use of their words in this book. We hope that omissions or errors will be called to our attention so that we can remedy them in future printings.

Grateful acknowledgment is made to the following: *Circus: An Investigation into What Makes the Sawdust Fly* by Alan Wykes. Copyright ©1977 Jupiter Books. *The Fool and His Scepter: A Study in Clowns and Jesters and Their Audience* by William Willeford. Copyright ©1969 by William Willeford. *Clowns* by John H. Towsen. Copyright ©1976 by John H. Towsen. *Bring on the Clowns* by Beryl Hugill. Copyright ©1980 Beryl Hugill. *Jung and Tarot: An Archetypal Journey* by Sallie Nichols. Copyright ©1980 Sallie Nichols. Used by permission of Samuel Weiser, Inc. *Harlequin, or The Rise and Fall of a Bergamask Rogue* by Thelma Niklaus. Copyright ©1956 Thelma Niklaus. *Grock: King of Clowns* by Grock [Adrien Wettach]. Copyright ©1957 Adrien Wettach. *The Great God Pan* by Robert Payne. Copyright ©1952 Robert Payne. *Center Ring: The People of the Circus* by Robert Lewis Taylor. Copyright ©1956 Robert Lewis Taylor. *The World of Clowns* by George Bishop. Copyright ©1976 George Bishop. *Fellini on Fellini* by Federico Fellino. English translation copyright ©1976 Eyre Methuen Ltd. *Life's a Lark* by Grock [Adrien Wettach]. Copyright ©1931 Adrien Wettach. *Dwarfs and Jesters in Art* by Erica Tietze-Conrat. Copyright ©1957 Erica Tietze-Conrat. *Here Come the Clowns* by Lowell Swortzell. Copyright ©1978 Lowell Swortzell. Used by permission of Viking Penguin Inc. *Clown Alley* by Bill Ballantine. Copyright ©1982 Bill Ballantine. *The Praise of Folly* by Desiderius Erasmus. Translation copyright ©1941 by Hoyt Hopewell Hudson. Used by permission of Princeton University Press. *A Seat at the Circus* by Antony Hippisley Coxe. Copyright ©1980 Antony Hippisley Coxe. *The Fool: His Social and Literary History* by Enid Welsford. Copyright ©1935 Enid Welsford. *Stages of the Clown: Perspectives on Modern Fiction from Dostoyevsky to Beckett* by Richard Pearce. Copyright ©1970 by Southern Illinois University Press. Reprinted by permission of the Southern Illinois University Press. "Laughter" by Henri Bergson. From *Comedy: An Essay on Comedy* by George Meredith. "Laughter" by Henri Bergson edited by Wylie Sypher. Copyright ©1956 Wylie Sypher. *Slapstick and Dumbbell—A Casual Survey of Clowns and Clowning* by Hiler Harzberg and Arthur Moss. Copyright ©1924 Harzberg and Moss. *Agee on Film* by James Agee. Copyright ©1958 the James Agee Trust. *Clowns and Pantomimes* by M. Willson Disher. Copyright ©1925, 1968 M. Willson Disher. *Funny People* by Steve Allen. Copyright ©1981 Steve Allen. *Joe Grimaldi: His Life and Theatre* by Richard Findlater [Kenneth Bain]. Copyright ©1955, 1978 Richard Findlater. *The English Circus* by Ruth Manning-Sanders. Copyright ©1952 Ruth Manning-Sanders. *Clown* by Emmett Kelly with F. Beverly Kelley. Copyright ©1954 Prentice-Hall, Inc. *A Passage to India* by E.M. Forster. Copyright ©1924 Harcourt, Brace and World, Inc.; copyright ©1952 E.M. Forster. *The Fool and the Trickster: Studies in Honor of Enid Welsford* by Paul V.A. Williams, editor. Copyright ©1979 by individual contributors. *The Book of Clowns* by George Speaight. Copyright ©1980 Roxby Press Productions, Ltd. *Here Comes the Circus* by Peter Verney. Copyright ©1978 Peter Verney. *The Last Days of Mr. Punch* by D.H. Myers. Copyright ©1971 D.H. Myers. *Parzival* by Wolfram von Eschenbach. Translation copyright ©1961 Helen M. Mustard and Charles E. Passage. *Fools and Folly: During the Middle Ages and the Renaissance* by Barbara Swain. Copyright ©1932 Columbia University Press. *Circus: A World History* by Rupert Croft-Cooke and Peter Cotes. Copyright ©1976 Paul Elek, Ltd. *Here We Are Again: Recollections of an Old Circus Clown* by Robert Sherwood. Copyright ©1926 Bobbs-Merrill Co. *Reality in a Looking-Glass: Rationality Through an Analysis of Traditional Folly* by Anton C. Zijderveld. Copyright ©1982 Anton C. Zijderveld. *Behind the Big Top* by David Lewis Hammarstrom. Copyright ©1980 A.S. Barnes and Co., Inc. *The History of Court Fools* by Dr. Doran. Copyright ©1966 Haskell House. *Circus Tales* by Edward Fitchner. Copyright ©1907 Hardpole and Comp. *Chipperfield's Circus* by P.M. Morris. Copyright ©1957 Faber and Faber. *Broken Hearted Clown* by Butch Reynolds. Copyright ©1954 Arco Publishers, Ltd. *Pink Coat, Spangles, and Sawdust* by Frank Foster. Copyright ©1948 Stanley Paul and Co., Ltd. *Showmen and Suckers* by M. Gorham. Copyright ©1951 Percival Marshall. *Circus Life and Amusements* by Charles Keith. Copyright ©1879 Bewley and Roe.

First Edition • Third Printing
A Star & Elephant Book
The Green Tiger Press, Inc.
San Diego, California
92101
Paperbound ISBN 0-914676-88-1

CONTENTS

FOREWORD

In this brief study I have addressed the various aspects
of the fool/clown in separate thematic chapters,
using "fool," "clown," and "jester" as virtually
synonymous terms throughout the book
to denote not only the professional
clown but the archetypal clown—
the fool who lurks in us all.

—Paul Cline

INTRODUCTION

In the hushed moments before the curtain rises, or the circus *entrée* begins, we sit in tense anticipation. As the clowns leap in, we tingle with a kind of pleasurable fear and smile a little in gleeful condescension before we settle back to enjoy the show, the exhibition of our follies.

From the moment man first laughed, the clown has been an inseparable part of the human spirit. And yet, we have always reacted to him with marked ambivalence. We seldom view a clown as a fellow human being, a three-dimensional personality like ourselves; we find it easier to see him as a capering bundle of nerves and energy, a mere human caricature. The professional clown, of course, encourages this perception. He conceals his true self behind a persona, his bizarre disguises automatically setting him apart as a quasi-human figure, a being who exists outside the bounds of normal society and normal responsibility, enjoying a freedom and license that the rest of us do not share.

Although we are sometimes made uncomfortable by the clown's grotesque exaggerations and grosser animal characteristics, these traits provide him with the necessary distance from the run of humanity that he—and his audience—requires. For though our appreciation of the clown's humor ultimately depends upon our ability to identify with the poor fool, we do not wish to be put into the uncomfortable position of empathising with the clown in the same way that we might empathise with a fellow human being in a painful or ludicrous situation. To one degree or another, distance and anonymity are essential to successful clowning. The clown must always seem physically, intellectually, and emotionally removed from us in some fundamental way; he must encourage us to suspend our normal sympathies so that we can fully enjoy the cathartic effects of unreserved and—let us admit it—somewhat malicious laughter. For the duration of the act, the clown must convince us that he is both more and less than human; he must successfully combine the polar traits of a ceremonial scapegoat figure and a particularly clever performing animal. "Why," we marvel, "he's almost human!"—a comment which aptly sums up our attitude towards this paradoxical creature of wonder and magic.

Today, in our pragmatic, scientific society, which demands prosaic explanations for everything and often seems bent on undermining our sense of mystery and wonder, there seems to be little we do not already know about the psychological significance of the fool/clown, the meanings of comedy, or the underlying causes of laughter. But not even the combined writings of Aristotle, Erasmus, Shakespeare, Bergson, Freud, and Jung have fully plumbed the mystery of the clown, and it is doubtful whether the research of psychologists, anthropologists, and social scientists will ever exhaust everything there is to know about the perennial fool. For the clown will never be reducible to mere definitions or to scientific formulae. He will merrily sidestep all our attempts to pin him down or categorize him. He will remain, for his sake and our own, forever elusive—forever contradictory.

However much we may deplore the excesses of clown humor—and the excesses of the clown have always been deplored—we will continue to find in it the anti-social, anarchic, and hilariously gross comedy that releases our frustrations and heals us with waves of unrestrained—and unrestrainable—laughter.

God bless the clown.

ORIGIN
AND
APPEARANCE

In Positano, Italy, I once saw a group of local youths stuff the pockets of the town's innocent—a poor, half-witted tramp—with paper, and then ignite it. After they doused the flaming and terrified creature with water, they took him off and bought him ice cream. Like the Positano tramp, the earliest tribal fools must have realized how their "innocence" could afford them a precarious means of survival in an otherwise hostile society—though they undoubtedly had to endure a few slaps from the hands that rewarded them. For we all feel generous towards those who can make us laugh, even though, and perhaps precisely because, they are so foolish. When we have plenty and are in good humor, we reward with magnanimous condescension the poor fool who is "not really fit to look after himself."

We cannot know with certainty how the clown evolved, but we do know that he has existed in virtually every human society. I cannot imagine even the smallest raggle-taggle, nut-, berry-, and root-gathering tribe without its own sort of clown. The clown in all his forms—from the American Indian trickster Coyote and the Chinese *ch'ou* to the Russian *Skomorokhi* and the English Joey—is an eternal human type, fulfilling universal and unchanging human needs. He has been with us since the very beginnings of human society, when the same impulses which gave rise to religious rituals and social hierarchies also generated the need for their antithesis: the propriety-smashing clown. When the tribal chiefs and their priests began to organize and restrict the actions of their people, we can well imagine the impertinent fool standing ever so slightly beyond the periphery of vision, imitating the leaders' officious gaits and gestures and mocking their religious rituals of suffering and abstention—and smiling ingenuously when he was finally caught out. And when man first began to daub his face with paints and dyes and adopt fantastical masks and costumes for his most solemn religious ceremonies, the awakening clown must surely have recognized the potential for disguises of a more profane kind.

We will probably never know how the clown wended his way from his lowly social position as a capering fool to his elevated status, in some societies, as a cathartic figure, given official sanction to act in shocking and scurrilous manners during important public ceremonies. Often exempt himself from the punishments that would surely have followed the ordinary citizens' identical transgressions, the clown was granted unheard of degrees of license, and soon found himself treading in the footsteps of the priests and shamans themselves, a key figure in their rites and festivals. And because he was granted such license, because he was not obliged to bow and scrape before the taboos and injunctions that bound his fellow citizens, the clown became, over time, a figure both exalted and ridiculed, a many-headed creature who was at once entertainer, social critic, healer, laughingstock, and scapegoat.

It is a long and not unbroken road from the tribal trickster and the ceremonial fool to the clown as we know him today. Along that road there have been many digressions and transformations. Over the centuries the clown has wandered from the villages of the common people to the courts of the rich and royal, and back again. He has known both the freedom of street improvisation and the discipline of theatrical routine and circus tradition. Our modern clowns in all their guises are not so much outgrowths as composites of all the jesters and harlequins, mountebanks and Merry Andrews, whitefaces and Augustes who have preceded them. Throughout the changing centuries, the essence of the clown has not changed at all. As he was once a central folk figure in our harvest festivals and seasonal ceremonies, serving as a counterpoint to their solemnity and a commentator upon their significance, he is now an inescapable part of our popular culture, still acting as a check upon our individual and social ills. He is our scapegoat, "he who gets slapped," suffering every indignity that the human mind can conceive. He is our alter ego, vicariously acting out the unspoken desires that we could never hope to act on in reality. He is our critic, piercing through our cultural hypocrisies with well-aimed barbs. And he is our healer, enabling us to laugh at realities that could too easily make us weep.

From unknown and unknowable origins in prehistory the clown has become the familiar and enduring figure we know from movies and television, theatre and circus. Like any archetype, his essence is fixed but his forms are mutable, changing as he grows to meet expanding human needs. Whatever his origin, whatever the course of his future evolution, the clown, we can rest assured, will continue his bumbling but necessary progress through civilization.

She saw a clown, a living limb of nonsense. She saw something she loved as she loved her root, her giraffe leg, her crimson dress.

Mervyn Peake, *Titus Groan*

It is reasonable to assume that the first clowning was accidental and that the first clowns were sublimely unconscious as to just how funny they were.

Hiler Harzberg and Arthur Moss,
Slapstick and Dumbbell

The first clown was a "clod," a clodhopper, a witless oaf who in time learned cunning...but who at first was pitiful and in a sense miraculous, for the derangement of his mind was a visitation from God. His antics, like those of the Fool in the Morris Dance, had a lunatic logic of their own that could not be shared by a more rational—allegedly more rational—people, who were awestruck by the uncomfortable thought that perhaps the pitiful clod was the only one in step with life.

Alan Wykes, *Circus!*

Thus it comes about that, in a world where men are differently affected toward each other, all are at one in their attitude toward these innocents; all seek them out, give them food, keep them warm, embrace them, and give them aid, if occasion rises; and all grant them leave to say and do what they wish, with impunity. So true it is that no one wishes to hurt them that even wild beasts, by a certain natural sense of their innocence, will refrain from doing them harm. They are indeed held sacred by the gods, especially by me; and not impiously do all men pay such honor to them.

Desiderius Erasmus, *The Praise of Folly*

The fool has antecedents and relatives among a wide range of people who in various ways violate the human image and who come to a modus vivendi *with society by making a show of that violation.*

William Willeford, *The Fool and His Scepter*

The fool's characteristic traits are very much those of "natural man." Lacking social graces and blissfully operating outside the laws of logic, he is often seen as a child or even an animal, but only rarely as a mature adult—his perceptions are too crudely structured, his use of language a parody of normal speech. Unimpressed with sacred ceremonies or the power of rulers, he is liable to be openly blasphemous and defiant; uninhibited in sexual matters, he often delights in obscene humor.

John H. Towsen, *Clowns*

In the cities of Megara and Sparta in Southern Greece...the clown...would wear tights, a short tunic or chiton *with half sleeves and would be grotesquely padded back and front; an exaggerated artificial phallus would be strapped round his loins. His shaven head glistened and his face was daubed with paint or soot...the clowns wore masks with yawning open mouths....Some clowns wore animal heads—the most popular of which was the cock's head....* (An allusion to vanity, stupidity, libidity, lascivity, and awareness.)

Beryl Hugill, *Bring on the Clowns*

In the theatre of Attic Greece the players were too far from the spectators to express emotion through the features. As with the clowns' makeup, exaggeration was necessary. A mask with thick upturned lips and another with the lips pursed and dropping could unmistakably signal comedy and tragedy, however great the distance. Colour helped: purple and blue and white for the draperies of those portraying the heavies; red and yellow or quarterings of several colours for those engaged in light relief or comedy. The symbolism persists to this day, as may be seen in any representation of a court jester's costume, which, with its Punchinello cap and bells, is an instant symbol for laughter. Motley and the mask, like the red nose and the white suit, have become immediately recognizable as simulations of all emotions needed to fit the story-line.

Alan Wykes, *Circus!*

The misshapenness of dwarfs, hunchbacks, and other grotesques is reflected in the dress of the fool, which characteristically contains chaotic and disproportionate elements but sometimes brings them together within a balanced and harmonious pattern.

William Willeford, *The Fool and His Scepter*

"What's your occupation?"
"Fool."

George Carlin

Dosennus was the cunning, wise fool character...the forerunner of Punch....A rather frightening hump-backed figure, he had a row of large teeth in a wide grinning mouth, a long hooked nose and an exaggerated jaw.... ...Stupidus was the Latin word for a mimic fool...he would be bald-headed... or wear a long pointed hat and a multi-colored outfit of which the later Harlequin costume must be a direct descendant.

Beryl Hugill, *Bring on the Clowns*

God touched the fool in many ways. In bygone times bodily deformities were looked upon as a special mark of the Lord; so dwarfs, hunchbacks, and the clubfooted were often chosen to be fools at court or in royal houses. Sometimes, ambitious parents even created such deformities by binding or other means, so that their offspring might aspire to the coveted position of the fool. Regardless of whether these maimed ones were touched by the miraculous hand of God or by the underhanded tricks of man, they often proved to be human beings of unusual depth and wisdom....

Sallie Nichols, *Jung and Tarot*

The earliest of the Fool Companies, called Les Enfants Sans Souce, was supposed to have originated toward the end of the fourteenth century...founded on the splendid principle that the world was mad and all men fools....All members wore the established fool's costume in public.

Hiler Harzberg and Arthur Moss, *Slapstick and Dumbbell*

And the queen thought further, "People are much given to mockery. Fool's clothing shall my child wear on his fair body. If he is pommeled and beaten, perhaps he will come back to me again." ...The lady took sack cloth and cut for him shirt and breeches which, all of a piece, came halfway down his white leg. Such was the regular garb of fools. On top was a hood, while from a hide of untanned calfskin boots were cut for his feet.

Wolfram von Eschenbach, *Parzival*

For my wish...I desire most marvellous things; just a fine bauble and a hood garnished with long ears and bells that make a marvellous noise....

Recueil de Poesies Francaises

The hood attached to the cloak was the covering for a fool, with an addition signified in a remark of Erasmus, that the Franciscans only wanted asses' ears and bells, to look like fools by profession. The Franciscans would seem to have intended some such profession, for they called themselves Mundi Moriones, *or* Fools of the World.

Dr. Doran, *The History of Court Fools*

The clown's image may at times approach that of a fearsome supernatural figure, but he is also a laughable buffoon, a fool whose message is delivered in an enjoyable form.

John H. Towsen, *Clowns*

Clowns maintain their distinctive characteristics despite, not because of tradition....These are...not borrowed but spontaneously created afresh.

William Willeford, *The Fool and His Scepter*

Arlecchino's complete presentation is one of the most perfect costumes ever conceived for the theatre, conveying immediately the mystery of his generation, the enigma of his personality, the haunting resemblances to ancient tradition, and his own prosaic, rustic reality. If his mask is not to be derived from the sooty faces or African masks of the phallophores and mimes, then it is terrifying in its implications, with its thick coarse brows over deep eye-sockets, with the heavy furrows along the narrow forehead outlining the astonished brow, the heavy pouches under the minute eyeholes, the vivid impression of sensuality and cunning, of diabolism and bestiality. It is repulsive and attractive. It takes us far beyond the Satyrs and the African slaves, into the darkness of mankind's primal imagination, back to the primitive emergence of man from the beast, reminding us that the beast still lurks within the man.

Thelma Niklaus, Harlequin, or The Rise and Fall of a Bergamask Rogue

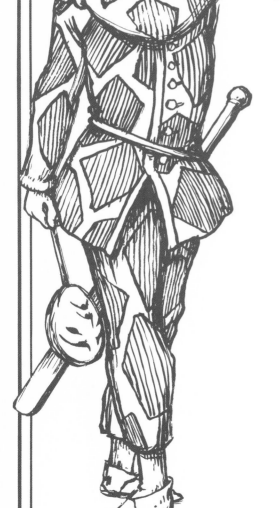

I decided to create a style of my own....One day I discovered in an old clothes shop the costume you all know. (The auguste's too-small jacket, huge trousers and shoes, and an absurd kind of clerical hat.)

Grock (Adrien Wettach), Grock: King of Clowns

Although Chaplin never worked in a circus, his tramp disguise links him to traditional circus clowning. The absurd contrasts which the circus clown employs are seen in the incongruity of the tiny bowler and the big, flapping shoes, the tight dinner jacket and the huge, baggy trousers.

Beryl Hugill, Bring on the Clowns

[Emmett] Kelly was dressed in a baggy brown suit of infinite tatters, large and leaky shoes, and a derby irretrievably lost to the world of fashion....His expression was so bedraggled and hopeless....The audience looked on with delight.

Robert Lewis Taylor, Center Ring

The younger brother spreads out the wide trousers of his costume, gay complex painted in every colour with the phases of the moon, with stars, whiskey bottles, jacks of cards, triangles, cubes, and the signs of the zodiac. He hopes I admire it; Paquin made it for him.

S. Young, "The Fratellini," New Republic, July 23, 1924

Grimaldi's uniform consisted of a wig with three black tufts in imitation of the dandy of Napoleonic days who wore his wig brushed down the back and tied the ends in a silk bag. Then there was a lace collar, a white tunic embroidered with scarlet circles or roses, silk hose with clocks and scarlet shoes and bright red garters at the knees. The face was painted dead white with here and there a few scarlet smears. Grimaldi explained that the scarlet smears and the large scarlet mouth were designed to give the effect of a boy who had been caught smearing his face with jam.

Robert Payne, The Great God Pan

What a face he had! The eyes large and globular and sparkling, and rolling, mostly, in a riot of joy; the nose, rudder of the soul, and almost always missing on actors, was on Grimaldi both noble and mobile beyond description; and oh! the capacious mouth, inside of which was a tongue ever vibrating, and below it, the chin that he had the power of lowering we will not say to what button of the waistcoat, but the drop was an alarming one.

D.H. Myers, The Last Days of Mr. Punch

Not very surprisingly, clowns feel fiercely protective about their makeup and costume inventions. The circus code forbids any plagiarism of these properties but is somewhat more lenient in the matter of gags. Clowns have been known to leave their "faces" to their families....

Robert Lewis Taylor, Center Ring

A clown face is hard to come by; it is the result of years of trial and error, of suggestions from fellow clowns, of observed reactions from audiences. Once it is set, it not only serves as a mark of identity but it conforms to the facial structure so that it looks natural in the sense that it doesn't intrude itself on the clown's normal features. A professional clown's face changes constantly during the early years of his development, sometimes not becoming definitely established until relatively late in his career.

George Bishop, The World of Clowns

I have already told of the first time I saw a circus and the first time I saw the clown, Pierino, at the fountain in the morning after the show....There is no doubt at all that he was the first herald of my unmistakeable vocation....I was moved and I admired the poor man dressed as a funny man, whom I realized was a free, amazing being, needing very little to live on and able to survive the most incredible disasters, able to rise from the most frightful calamities, pass unharmed through mockery and contempt and to the very end maintain an unflagging optimism: amused and amusing as only one under heaven's protection could possibly be.

Federico Fellini, Fellini on Fellini

During the entire afternoon the young fry of the village stood glued to the spot witnessing the exciting procedure of the tent pegs being driven into the ground and the canvas being fixed to the great pole. Imagine our ecstasy when night fell and upon the platform erected in front of the tent the artists paraded in the glare of the naphtha lamps, inciting the public to enter by their jokes and their antics. The troupe consisted mainly of seven children in rose-red tights, with a big, jovial man at their head, with a white-chalked face and scarlet nose and mouth. For the first time in my life I beheld a CLOWN, and for the first time also felt something stir within me that was not just mere childhood excitement. That something said to me: I WILL. I will become what that man is there upon the platform.

Grock (Adrien Wettach), *Life's a Lark*

She picked up the last card, that numbered nought, and exhibited it. It might have needed some explanation, for it was obscure enough. It was painted with the figure of a young man, clothed in an outlandish dress of four striped colours —black and grey and silver and red; his legs and feet and arms and hands were bare, and he had over one shoulder a staff, carved into serpentine curves, that carried a round bag, not unlike the balls with which the Juggler played. The bag rested against his shoulder, so that as he stood there he supported as well as bore it. Before him a dragon-fly, or some such airy creature, danced; by his side a larger thing, a lynx or young tiger, stretched itself up to him—whether in affection or attack could not be guessed, so poised between both the beast stood. The man's eyes were very bright; he was smiling, and the smile was so intense and rapt that those looking at it felt a quick motion of contempt—no sane man could be as happy as that.

Charles Williams, *The Greater Trumps*

13

WISDOM
AND FOLLY

In his sixteenth-century essay, *The Praise of Folly*, Erasmus explores the image of the self-proclaimed wise man who, smugly secure in his intelligence and wisdom, points a disparaging finger at the supposedly inferior fool. The fool, after all, cannot disguise his foolishness; in his speech and by his actions he is clearly, recognizably, a fool. The fool, for his part, is unaware of his own folly, and he delights in mocking the pretensions of the wise man. For while it is true that a genuine fool cannot feign wisdom, neither can the truly wise man deny the elements of folly in his own nature. If he attempts to do so, then he becomes the very thing that he most fears becoming: a fool.

There is a kind of wisdom that goes beyond the intellect, a subconscious or pre-conscious knowing that is the province not of the disciplined thinker but of the instinctual fool. For centuries, the fool was regarded not merely as a figure of fun but also as a being under heaven's protection, a creature privy to secrets denied other men. The "moonstruck" fool often had the edge over more conventional sages, and in royal courts throughout the world he often enjoyed a substantial influence over his masters, his special status affording him a greater freedom and license than that granted to the king's own lords and ministers. Nor were court fools always or even usually mad or mentally deficient. According to one famous legend, when the cruel and obsessive Chou dynasty emperor Shih Huang-ti decided to volunteer his subjects for the suicidal task of painting the Great Wall of China, it was his personal clown, Yu Sze, who subtly but successfully humored him out of his outrageous ambition.

The natural fool—the actual simpleton—is an innocent and ignorant creature. The professional clown, however, is no innocent, and his ignorance is feigned, his foolishness calculated. His success depends on a rich background of personal experience combined with a native cleverness and insight which allow him to learn and work within the traditions of his craft. The clown must be artist and actor, philosopher and psychologist. He is surely no fool; he deals in counterfeit folly. And, as Shakespeare's Viola notes in *Twelfth Night*, "to do that well craves a kind of wit."

There are times when folly—or the recognition that folly exists within each of us—is the supreme form of wisdom. In the clown act the audience is invited to confront its own follies, and to laugh in recognition of them. The clown does not deliberately set out to teach, any more than we seek to learn from him. But the laughter that a great clown can elicit from us sets into motion some inner mechanism of insight and growth, and in the unreflective spontaneity of our reactions some essential force is liberated. More than the teachings of a wise man, the actions of the fool serve once more to show us that folly can be, after all, the most sublime expression of wisdom.

The most exquisite folly is made of wisdom spun too fine.

Benjamin Franklin

The folly of clowns should always be the bouquet of long and slowly gathered wisdom.

James Agate

Nay, I shall ne'er be ware of mine own wit till I break my shins against it.

Shakespeare, As You Like It

If any here chance to behold himself, let him not dare to challenge me of wrong; for, if he shame to have his follies known, first he should shame to act 'em. My strict hand was made to seize on vice, and with a gripe, squeeze out the humor of such spongy natures as lick up every idle vanity.

Ben Jonson, Every Man Out of His Humour

The custom of having a joker at table has been observed throughout the centuries...the jester who can make a joke, or even one who knows how to tell a good one, is no fool; and to have to make merry, to improve someone else's digestion, invites criticism. He must eat less, dance less, womanize less; the fool condemns such frivolous pursuits. The fool is the sage who says "Vanitas Vanitatum" to all that.

Erica Tietze-Conrat, Dwarfs and Jesters in Art

It was the function of the king's jester to remind him of his follies, of the mortality of all men, and to help him guard against the sin of hubris, or overweening pride.

Sallie Nichols, Jung and Tarot

Yet even when our folly becomes dangerously swollen with pride, it contains the possibility that the fool will illumine our darkness in a spontaneous show. It is the possibility that his show, replacing the light by which we usually understand and act, will free us from the dead forms of what we foolishly thought was life.

William Willeford, The Fool and His Scepter

...the fool was permitted to do or say pretty much what he pleased—a freedom that other subjects must have envied. The fool spoke his mind with embarrassing frankness; empty flattery and tedious ritual were favorite targets for his pointed wit. Acting as an informal master of ceremonies, he was free to cut short a courtier's windy speech or a councilor's boring discourse, and this made him a powerful figure at court. The fool was permitted these remarkable liberties because, in turn, he allowed the king himself a kind of liberation from the stifling etiquette of his own court.

Lowell Swortzell, Here Come the Clowns

Seest thou a wise man in his own conceit? There is more hope for a fool than of him.

Proverbs

If any man among you seemeth to be wise to this world, let him become a fool, that he may be wise.

Paul, *I Corinthians iii, 18*

Men are so necessarily foolish that not to be a fool is merely a varied freak of folly.

Blaise Pascal

Foolery, sir, does walk about the orb like the sun; it shines everywhere.

Shakespeare, *Twelfth Night*

He appears from some point of view erring and irresponsible. He transgresses or ignores the code of reasoned self-restraint under which society attempts to exist, is unmeasured in his hilarity or in his melancholy, disregards the logic of cause and effect and conducts himself in ways which seem rash and shocking to normal mortals.

Barbara Swain, *Fools and Folly*

In some Tarot cards the Fool is pictured as blindfolded, further emphasizing his ability to act by insight rather than eyesight, using intuitive wisdom instead of conventional logic.

Sallie Nichols, *Jung and Tarot*

Behind our backs, but before our grinning faces, the clown continues to do what has kept him a significant force for morality. By keeping man in perspective with his times, the clown acts as a powerful corrective; he points out the breed of animal that lies under our often hypocritical hides. Grist for the clown mill is anything that shows men and women as less than perfect. Clowns point up frustration, failure, and ineptitude.

Bill Ballantine, *Clown Alley*

For what that passes among mortals everywhere is not full of folly, done by fools in the presence of fools?

Desiderius Erasmus, *The Praise of Folly*

Were it not for bunglers in the manner of doing it, hardly any man would ever find out he was laughed at.

Lord Halifax

The fool as opposed to the wise man has one advantage from the outset, in that he is incapable of glorying in his wisdom, as the wise man is always tempted to do.

Erica Tietze-Conrat, *Dwarfs and Jesters in Art*

Only a fool would think of imitating...another person and only another fool would be deceived by the imitation. The same interplay between the fool and himself...may be seen in the device of the fool pair...Lear and his fool, Don Quixote and Sancho Panza...one of the pair is usually the knave or wit, the other the dupe or butte; the two often exchanging roles back and forth in a flood of surprises.

William Willeford, *The Fool and His Scepter*

Sometimes the Fool, depicted more outspokenly as the king's counterpart, is shown wearing a crown. A crown is symbolically a golden halo, open at the top to receive illumination from above. Thus, both king and fool are seen to be divinely inspired. As the king ruled by divine right, so his counterpart had a right equally divine to criticize him and to offer challenging suggestions.

Sallie Nichols, *Jung and Tarot*

If I want to look at a fool, I have only to look in a mirror.

Seneca

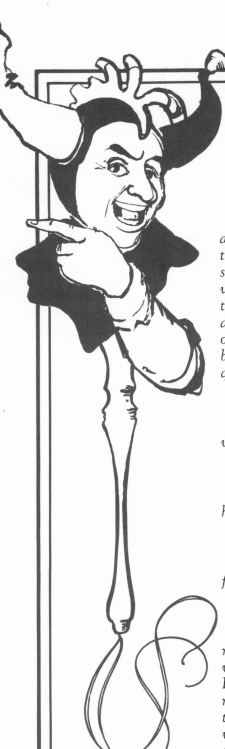

Jesters do oft prove prophets.

Shakespeare

Notice also this estimable gift of fools, that they alone are frank and ingenuous. What is more praiseworthy than truth?...Whatever a fool has in his heart, that he sets also in his face and utters in his speech. But your wise man has two tongues...one used for speaking truth, the other for speaking what he judges most opportune at the moment. Black is turned into white by these men of wisdom; they blow hot and cold with the same breath, and hidden in the breast they have something quite different from what they frame in speech.

Desiderius Erasmus, *The Praise of Folly*

If the fool would persist in his folly he would become wise.

William Blake

Every man's follies are the caricature resemblances of his wisdom.

John Sterling, *Essays and Tales*

The Fool, whoever and wherever he is, is not merely foolish.

Paul V.A. Williams, editor, *The Fool and the Trickster*

Like the foolhardy third brother in fairy tales who rushes in where angels fear to tread, and by doing so wins the hand of the princess and her kingdom, the Fool's spontaneous approach to life combines wisdom, madness, and folly. When he mixes these ingredients in the right proportions the results are miraculous, but when the mixture curdles, everything can end up in a sticky mess. At these times the Fool can look pretty foolish which (being a fool) he has the good sense not to mind. He is often pictured like Bottom, wearing asses' ears because he knows that to admit ignorance is the highest knowledge—the necessary condition of all learning.

Sallie Nichols, *Jung and Tarot*

"I would rather be as plain as you are and have some sense, than be as beautiful as I am and at the same time stupid."
"Nothing more clearly displays good sense, madam, than a belief that one is not possessed of it. It follows, therefore, that the more one has, the more one fears it to be wanting."

Charles Perrault, *Ricky of the Tuft*

A man who knows he is a fool is not a great fool.

Chuang-tse

He who lives without folly is hardly so wise as he thinks.

La Rouchefoucauld

Hence it appears that among mortals they who are zealous for wisdom are farthest from happiness, being by the same token fools twice over.

Desiderius Erasmus, *The Praise of Folly*

The fool is often like an infant in that the objects of his desire and aversion do not fit the patterns and desires of responsible adults.

William Willeford, *The Fool and His Scepter*

People are sentimental enough to prefer to link sorrow with the clown. They like to identify themselves with "he who gets slapped." Children love him for a simpler reason. He expresses, loudly and eloquently, the bewilderment they feel when they find themselves in an adult world. In showing up the ridiculous foibles of mankind he provides the young with the confirmation that it's pretty silly being grown-up anyway, and for that they adore him.

Antony Hippisley Coxe, *A Seat at the Circus*

O noble fool! A worthy fool! Motley's the only wear!

Shakespeare, *As You Like It*

In Comedy, the best actor plays the part of the droll, while some second rogue is made the hero or fine gentleman. So, in this farce of life, wise men pass their time in mirth, while fools only are serious.

Jonathan Swift

*I must have liberty
Withal, as large a charter as the wind,
To blow on whom I please; for so fools have.
And they that are most galled with my folly,
They most must laugh.*

Shakespeare, *As You Like It*

When a thing is funny search it for a hidden truth.

George Bernard Shaw

If the animals suddenly got the gift of laughter, they would begin by laughing themselves sick about man, that most ridiculous, most absurd, most foolish of all animals.

Egon Friedell

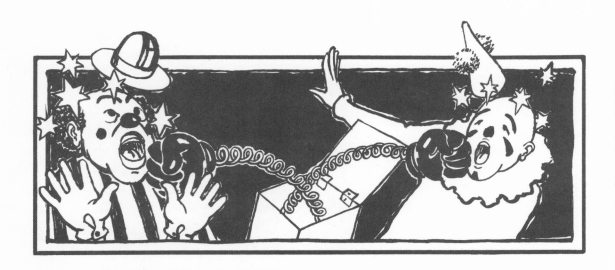

FOOLS AND
THE WORLD OF MATTER

"You can do some awful wild things with railroads," said Buster Keaton, after filming *The General*. This remark is a marvelous summation of the clown's attitude towards the physical world, the world of matter. Virtually every clown act relies to one degree or another on physical humor, on the fool's confrontations with malfunctioning objects or devices that cannot be mastered. With single-minded determination the clown withstands every obstacle that the world can hurl at him, sometimes turning the odds in his favor through sheer accident or blind persistence. His own unpredictable and anarchic nature is more than a match for the chaos he encounters in the world.

The clown is continually frustrated by the cause-and-effect world of matter. He often copes with this frustration through furious action, a sometimes desperate lashing-out that temporarily assuages his sense of outrage. When he is not actively and aggressively confronting the maddening trappings of an incomprehensible material world, he is passively submitting to it. And yet his very submission is a form of defiance, for in surrendering himself to chaos—a chaos that he ironically, through his ignorance and incompetence, helps to create—he demonstrates his superiority to mere physical laws. The clown survives all manner of abuse and mishap and emerges triumphant, immortal—and usually more or less intact.

The clown is not necessarily a courageous creature, but he is a fearless one, unable to conceive that he might possibly come to harm. Awareness of the true danger involved is left to the audience; the clown himself is protected by his ignorance. The clown's thinking is not deficient; his comedic solutions to problems often make a bizarre kind of sense. But he does not reason as we do. To him, the simple method is complex, the complex method merely the "logical" way to do things. Where we would use a flyswatter, he would use a Rube Goldberg contraption, with perhaps a few more gadgets added for good measure. And yet we cannot deny that the clown achieves results—perhaps by the most convoluted methods possible, and even then by accident—but he achieves them nevertheless.

The clown's dogged persistence—his foolhardy will—enables him to surmount obstacles that would defeat an ordinary mortal early in the game. The great clown routines of fools trapped in and dealing with the world of matter represent the triumph of human will and laughter over the impersonal forces of the machine and the frightening unpredictability of nature. As we laugh, we are acknowledging the elements of chance and circumstance that can upset the order of our lives at any moment. But we are also recognizing the largely illusory nature of that order, and the power of human will and instinct to transform mischances into happy accidents.

The battle is from the outset one-sided, the fools against a horrible force which would defeat us if we were in their places.

William Willeford, *The Fool and His Scepter*

Many of the prize dreams of childhood are accomplished by the clown before one's very eyes: the breaking of vast quantities of crockery; the wholesale swallowing of enormous pastries; the discomfiting of policemen and other such pompous asses; and the burlesqueing of parents, classic dancers and musicians, strong men, and other pretentious bores.

Hiler Harzberg and Arthur Moss, *Slapstick and Dumbbell*

...whenever the clown baffles the policeman, whenever the fool makes the sage look silly, whenever the acrobat defeats the machine, there is a sudden sense of pressure relieved, of a birth of new joy and freedom.

Enid Welsford, *The Fool*

It is, in fact, probable that we are laughing not only at [the clowns'] inappropriate and pedantic fuming but also at their dedication to the meaningful continuance of life. There is, as well, something sinister about their heroism. Their participation in the human image, already slight because they are clowns, is violated further and further until we must realize that it is not the human will that is in them enduring and even holding its own against chaos; there seems, rather, to be a secret collaboration between them and whatever is attacking them. They go on being tormented as mice by a cat; if we were the mice, we would have given ourselves up much sooner! The fact that the fools permit, without succumbing to panic and running, makes us begin to respect that a single intelligence, like that of an unimaginable cat-mouse, is playing with us through them, through their dilemma, and through their attempts to deal with it.

William Willeford, *The Fool and His Scepter*

I have many a time had an unlucky fall, or gone through a performance with my knee out of place, and rushed out of the ring limping with pain, thus causing a call back, for the comic way in which the audience thought I had acted.

Charlie Keith, *Circus Life and Amusements*

[Grimaldi] was a glutton who would swallow strings of sausages and platefuls of tarts—props he has passed on to the modern circus clown....Many of the jokes Grimaldi invented were entirely original and depended mainly on constructing things out of unlikely objects. He would turn himself into a hussar by donning coal-scuttle "boots," candlestick "spurs," and red pantaloons.... Throughout his career he suffered broken bones, wrenched muscles and other injuries brought on by numberless comic kicks and beatings...once when an unloaded pistol triggered off when he was pulling it from his boot in a mock fight, thus setting fire to his stocking, he played on to the end of the performance....On another occasion... Grimaldi was supposed to shoot up through a trapdoor in the stage; but the ropes holding him snapped and he fell back, hurting himself badly on the hard cellar floor.

Beryl Hugill, *Bring on the Clowns*

The world of inanimate objects has always been friendly towards me. Malicious I have never found them. Years ago I was in Barcelona when an anarchist wanted to blow up the cafe with a bomb. The bomb was placed beneath my chair. I could sniff the lighted fuse, and, groping under my seat, I picked up the abortion, that promptly began to purr like a cat and quite forgot to go off.

Grock (Adrien Wettach), *Life's a Lark*

The many stories of clowns being injured, often seriously, by their own props and gadgets, and yet continuing their performance, speak not only of their courage and their determination to prove the maxim that "the show must go on," but also of something much deeper in their nature: a staunch refusal to allow any reversal to darken their essential world of clownery, to overcome their bright spirit.

A fool is an automaton. He is a machine worked by a spring. Irresistible natural forces make him move and turn, always at the same pace and never stopping. He is never inconsistent with himself. Whoever has seen him once has seen him at all times. He is fixed and immovable by nature.

Jean de la Bruyere, *Caracteres XI*

Perhaps one reason that the clown has appealed to the Romantic imagination is that he demonstrates the ultimate Romantic affirmation. By deliberately truning himself into a puppet with innumerable conflicting parts, he frees himself to react most fully to his environment. By deliberately displacing his center of gravity and orientation from his head, he frees himself from the control of rational purpose, and he frees himself to create and define his environment. By turning himself into a machine, he achieves a final victory over the world of machines.

Richard Pearce, *Stages of the Clown*

... clowns came and went, collided, fell and jumped up again in a uniformly accelerated rhythm, visibly intent upon effecting a crescendo. *And it was more and more to the jumping up again, the* rebound, *that the attention of the public was attracted. Gradually, one lost sight of the fact that they were men of flesh and blood like ourselves; one began to think of bundles of all sorts, falling and knocking against each other. Then the vision assumed a more definite aspect. The forms grew rounder, the bodies rolled together and seemed to pick themselves up like balls. Then at last appeared the image towards which the whole of this scene had doubtless been unconsciously evolving —large rubber balls hurled against one another in every direction. The second scene, though even coarser than the first, was no less instructive. There came on the stage two men, each with an enormous head, bald as a billiard ball. In their hands they carried large sticks which each, in turn, brought down on the other's cranium. Here, again, a certain gradation was observable. After each blow, the bodies seemed to grow heavier and more unyielding, overpowered by an increasing degree of rigidity. Then came the return blow, in each case heavier and more resounding than the last, coming, too, after a longer interval. The skulls gave forth a formidable ring throughout the silent house. At last the two bodies, each quite rigid and as straight as an arrow, slowly bent over towards each other, the sticks came crashing down for the last time on to the two heads with a thud as of enormous mallets falling upon oaken beams, and the pair lay prone upon the ground. At that instant appeared in all its vividness the suggestion that the two artists had gradually driven into the imagination of the spectators: "We are about to become...we have now become solid wooden dummies."*

Henri Bergson, *Laughter*

Ever since I can remember, all kinds of inanimate objects have had a way of looking to me reproachfully and whispering to me in unguarded moments: "We've been waiting for you...at last you've come...take us now, and turn us into something different...we've been so bored, waiting...."

Grock (Adrien Wettach), Life's a Lark

A man whose life it is to turn somersaults and twist himself into knots, eat fire and ice and glass, to say nothing of the circus dust that must...fill his lungs, can't last like ordinary men. 'Tisn't everyone who's composed of barbed wire, as I am. He must have as much recoil in him as a Parabellum pistol.

Grock (Adrien Wettach), *Life's a Lark*

When [Keaton] moved his eyes, it was like seeing them move in a statue. His short-legged body was all sudden, machinelike angles, governed by a daft aplomb. When he swept a semaphorelike arm to a point, you could almost hear the electrical impulse in the signal block. When he ran from a cop his transitions from accelerating walk to easy jogtrot to brisk canter to headlong gallop to flogged-piston sprint...were as distinct and as soberly in order as an automatic gearshift.

James Agee, *Agee on Film*

Grock spent most of his career polishing a single entree, and over the years his solos increased. He not only became more of an eccentric, he grew to be more of a mime as well. His movements and gestures became so well timed and choreographed that his performance was often compared to the precise yet complex products of the watchmakers of his native Switzerland.

John H. Towsen, *Clowns*

[Grock's] performance, which invited sympathy yet indicated triumph at one and the same time, was unique. He waddled on to the stage with a self-deprecating manner carring a huge leather portmanteau, out of which he pulled the tiniest of fiddles. He tuned this instrument by blowing up a green balloon, which he then held by the neck to let the air slowly out to produce a perfect E. The audience would long to rush to help him as he struggled to right the violin and bow which had somehow got into the wrong hands....One of his most inspired pieces of business was to move the piano to the chair instead of the chair to the piano....[It does sound rather simple, as most clown routines do in black and white, but after seeing it on television—surely a pale representation of the live act—I can truthfully say that it is superb.]

None of the clown's traditional booby traps overcame Grock....He seemed to run into them with a kind of exultation.

Beryl Hugill, *Bring on the Clowns*

Grock, like Grimaldi, is the funnier the deeper one pries into his soul. He also stands among commonplace materials and his wonder makes them like the sun and stars. His piano is enlarged into man's eternal struggle with fate. His fiddle and bow express all the hopes, trials, despairs, and joys that have ever been encountered and overcome. His chair is raised to the importance of Cassiopeia's. His fall through the seat of it shakes our belief in the security of the universe. Life is full of pitfalls, is his philosophy. Life, he implies, would be very dull if it were not. Yes, undoubtedly, he is profound.

M. Willson Disher, *Clowns and Pantomimes*

There's something about my profession that's irresistible, or so I think—this mastering by willpower, this transforming the little everyday annoyances, not only overcoming, but actually transforming them into something strange and terrific.

Grock (Adrien Wettach), *Life's a Lark*

Whatever the task at hand, the clown usually will exert a tremendous amount of misguided energy and, more often than not, accomplish very little. His methods are as inappropriate as his failure is predictable.

John H. Towsen, *Clowns*

When the clown stood apart from the main action, there was a balance between his world and the world from which he stood apart—between appearance and reality, the ideal and the actual....But with the clown at the center of the action the equilibrium and balance are destroyed. Appearance and reality, the ideal and the actual blend and mix.

Richard Pearce, *Stages of the Clown*

The magical force that induces chaos in the presence of the fool...is illustrated by a scene from W.C. Field's film The Bank Dick (1940). Fields drives a car at great speed while a bank robber in the seat behind him points a gun at him; they are chased by policemen on motorcycles. In the course of the pursuit, the controlling mechanisms of the car begin to disintegrate. Unperturbed, Fields throws away the gearshift and the brakes and passes the steering wheel to the robber. The car careens madly but without accident, dodging obstacles, until it finally comes to a halt at the very edge of a cliff. Fields steps out, the criminal having passed out with fright, to be greeted as a hero by the arriving police. [That] the magical power that guides the car...belongs to the fool or...he belongs to it is shown by the fact that Fields takes the astonishing course of events completely for granted and that it ends in a triumph for him.

William Willeford, *The Fool and His Scepter*

Sennett's comedies were just a shade faster and fizzier than life....Realizing the tremendous drumlike power of mere motion to exhilarate, he gave inanimate objects a mischievous life of their own, broke every law of nature the tricked camera would serve him for, and made the screen dance like a witches' Sabbath. The thing one is surest of all to remember is how toward the end of nearly every Sennett comedy, a chase (usually called "the rally") built up such a majestic trajectory of pure anarchic motion that bathing girls, cops, comics, dogs, cats, babies, automobiles, locomotives, innocent bystanders, sometimes what seemed like a whole city, an entire civilization, were hauled along head over heels in the wake of that energy like dry leaves following an express train.

James Agee, *Agee on Film*

The fool is often clumsy as well as stupid. He is lacking, that is to say, in his ability to perceive, understand, or act in accordance with the order of things as it appears to others. His perception, understanding, and actions are thus relatively uncoordinated, even chaotic. What he says and does seems symptomatic of an inadequacy or aberration. He has difficulties with physical objects, with social forms, and with the rules that govern both. These difficulties and his failure to master them result in what strikes us as a ridiculous loss of dignity. Often, however, he does not feel the pain and embarrassment that such oddity and failure would cause in us—he may even be proud of them; in any case, his notions of what constitutes accomplishment are different from ours.

William Willeford, *The Fool and His Scepter*

The liberty horses have left the ring. The last of the carpet clowns with a couple of flip-flaps and a final caper have followed them. The music changes tempo and a single light illuminates a shuffling figure as he makes his way with some pretense of dignity to the center of the sawdust. He wears a long top coat of an outrageous tweed which is far too big for him and all but sweeps the ground. Around his neck is an open white collar and a wisp of a black bow tie. His face is white and he has on a floppy shapeless hat over his bald pate. On his feet is a pair of outsize shoes and on his back he carries an enormous trunk.

This strange figure walks into the middle of the ring, seemingly unconscious of the total concentration of five thousand pairs of eyes watching his every movement, or of the ripple of excited anticipation which followed his entrance. He seems uncertain about where to put down his great trunk and he wanders disconsolately round the ring with puzzlement and concern written all over him. At last he seems satisfied. With deliberate and exaggerated care he places the trunk on the ground and, with equal deliberation, opens it. He reaches in and brings out a tiny fiddle. As though pleased with his performance, his face, which had not so much as moved a muscle, breaks into a broad smile of greeting, and the audience roars. Grock the incomparable, King of Clowns, has arrived.

The smile is replaced with a frown of intense concentration. The maestro raises a hand, bidding silence. The huge audience stills. With the air of an accomplished performer, Grock places one foot on a chair. The ridiculous and diminutive violin is put to his cheek. With rapt attention he strums a string or two to tune it. He looks up to indicate that he is ready. With a flourish he throws his bow in the air intending to catch it, but misses as it falls to the ground. A gesture of annoyance, a frown creases the serene white face. He tries again and once more fails to catch the bow. With an imperious gesture, he summons a screen behind which he can practice. The audience, somewhat mystified by now, watches the bow rise above the screen and sees it fall again. Time and again Grock tries the trick. Small boys in the front rows can be seen biting their nails as they will him to succeed. The audience is hushed as though witness to a great event and all want the poor man to perform the feat which clearly means so much to him. At length, satisfied that now he can do it, Grock returns to the ring. He bows again to his audience as though thanking them for their consideration. He takes up his position by the chair again and with a beatific smile throws his bow in the air once more. It falls to the ground. Perplexed, his face strained with the effort, he studies it intently. He throws it up again. Once more it falls to the ground. In apparently sheer exasperation he hurls it toward the roof, twice as high as he has thrown it before, and as it falls he deftly catches it. His face lights up from ear to ear in a smile of the sheerest delight and the audience erupts.

Peter Verney, *Here Comes the Circus*

LAUGHTER IN THE FACE OF CHAOS AND TRAGEDY

The image of a broken-hearted or lovesick clown, bravely keeping up his comic facade in spite of deep personal pain, has long been a popular conception, although many professional clowns scoff at this romantic stereotype. In his private life the clown is no more likely to be happy or carefree than the average person, and certainly there have been many clowns with tragic personal histories. But no matter what the condition of his inner life, the clown knows that his business is to alleviate his audience's cares and concerns with laughter. He deflates our arrogance, pointing our attention away from tail-biting self-absorption and towards a healthy humility, a saner perspective that only the comic vision can give us. For how can anything be tragic, how can anything overwhelm us, if we can make fun of both it and ourselves, and, by the force of our laughter, reduce it to a mere wisp of smoke and blow it out the window with a gentle puff?

Many great thinkers throughout the ages have recognized how thin the line is that separates comedy from tragedy. The clown suggests that the essential difference between the two is merely a function, ultimately, of how we choose to view a given situation. The clown knows that it is easy enough to wallow in self-pity, to selectively focus on life's missed opportunities and thwarted desires. No earthly power can rid the world of accident and tragedy, but the clown, in his own humble way, attempts to redress the imbalance, to put the odds back in our favor. In his skilled hands, a natural disaster can be transformed into a comic inconvenience; a failed romance can be attributed to nothing more serious than clumsy feet, poor timing, or a conspicuous nose. In the clown's world, a man can be riddled with thirty bullets and feel nothing more than a tickling sensation; he can be clubbed, pummelled, and doused with water and yet suffer nothing more than outraged dignity. The clown, in all of these situations, champions the underdog; and each of us, in the face of chaos and tragedy, is at least a bit of an underdog. He allows us to feel, for a fleeting moment, that we have gained the upper hand at last.

The clown does not try to dominate or manipulate reality. He does not deny the existence of pain and tragedy. We see him meeting the world on its own terms, allowing it to use him and even beat him. And yet, when the act is over, we can acknowledge the clown as the victor. Perhaps this is because we recognize that it takes great courage to surrender to chaos—as it takes a great spirit to rise above tragedy.

I am forced to try to make myself laugh that I may not cry: for one or other I must do; and is it not philosophy carried to the highest pitch for a man to conquer such tumults of soul as I am sometimes agitated by, and in the very height of the storm to quaver out a horselaugh?

Samuel Richardson, *Clarissa*

The more one suffers, the more, I believe, one has a sense for the comic. It is only by the deepest suffering that one acquires the authority in the art of the Comic; an authority which by one word transforms as by magic the resoundable creature one calls man into a caricature.

Søren Kierkegaard

But the clown needs more than physical skills. He does not present us simply with the childish comic-strip humour of the man who bangs his nose after treading on a garden rake. He is also telling us something about our human condition. To do this he will need to have a deep experience of life. It seems no coincidence that most clowns have had deeply unhappy—or at least disrupted—childhoods. This early experience of hardship gives them a sense of the absurdity of life so necessary to a clown—as well as the capacity to deal with sorrow in later life.

Beryl Hugill, *Bring on the Clowns*

In private life clowns are not very talkative and are inclined to be moody. You have to know them well before their shyness and reserve can be broken through. They are philosophers and will discuss for hours how to get a laugh. When they perform in the ring they draw upon the rich experience of their varied lives. The greatest clowns have invariably been those with the widest experience.

Rupert Croft-Cooke, *The Circus Book*

The best humor, in my opinion, is found in the frequently tragic reality of human experience.

Steve Allen, *Funny People*

Slowly, painfully, quietly, Grimaldi walked on to the stage for the last time. He was dressed in black, with a white waistcoat and gloves. As he advanced towards the footlights, the other performers silently ranged themselves behind him, and he addressed the audience in a voice that was often rough with emotion. When he had finished, with tears streaming down his cheeks, the company moved towards him, and amid deafening applause the back scene was drawn off to reveal the manager's piece de resistance—a set of coloured lights arranged in the words GRIMALDI'S FAREWELL. After bowing and waving to the audience, Grimaldi was led off into the green room, and there he wept aloud "with an intensity of suffering that it was painful to witness and impossible to alleviate." He was in so disturbed and hysterical a state that he could not carry out his promise to distribute his farewell wardrobe as souvenirs among his friends, and after a few hurried goodbyes he was lifted into a coach and driven home to Exmouth Street.

Richard Findlater,
Joe Grimaldi: His Life and Theatre

*The saddest ones are those that wear
The jester's motley garb.*

D. Marquis

A jest breaks no bones.

Samuel Johnson, *Boswell's Life*

Everything is funny as long as it is happening to somebody else.

Will Rogers

29

Worn are my clothes almost out by being whipped and knocked about; Torn is my face in twenty places by stretching wide to make grimaces.

a Dick Dewhurst (English clown) song quoted in Ruth Manning-Sanders, *The English Circus*

Slivers Oakley complains, *"If people only would laugh at something nice and kind and gentle! But no—not for them! We have to kick and get kicked, punch and get punched, get up, fall down, roll around, and get generally walked all over, trampled under and hoofed up, to make any sort of hit at all.*

quoted in John H. Towsen, *Clowns*

I never saw anything funny that wasn't terrible. If it causes pain it's funny: if it doesn't, it isn't.

W.C. Fields

To become conscious of what is horrifying and to laugh at it is to become master of that which is horrifying....Laughter alone does not respect any taboo, laughter alone inhibits the creation of new anti-taboos; the comic alone is capable of giving us the strength to bear the tragedy of existence.

Eugene Ionesco

In a sense the two clowns enact the struggle of man against a "chaotic and cruel cosmos," but their enactment of it apparently has little to do with choice, responsibility, victory, or even learning anything. Their ignorance of the moral dimension is not at the moment bliss for them, but it allows them to go on, and it brings to us a sense of expansion, of freedom. The silliness and the sinister overtones do not lessen the heroism of the clowns, and our mockery at them does not lessen our admiration of them. We know that light, life and good are invaluable, that their victory demands sacrifice and may result in tragedy or, much worse, deliverance up to the demonic or simply to nothingness. The clowns remind us of a truth as ancient and as important: that light, life and good are not necessarily synonymous and that, in any case, they are not limited to conscious order.

William Willeford, *The Fool and His Scepter*

...Charlie [Chaplin] is...Pan alive, calling upon the earth and heavens to witness that he is alive and kicking. Half bird, half elephant, he lives in a universe which grows, as does Blake's, according to the acts of his imagination and in no other way. He is one of God's elect, but that disturbs him less than his knowledge of the evil of the world, and the folly of it, yet he goes out to encounter folly with the divine grace of Don Quixote. "He is chasing folly, and he knows it," Chaplin said once. "He is trying to meet the world bravely, to put up a bluff, and he knows that too." So he does, but the game is played unfairly, for he hides up his sleeve an armament of cards which he can snap upon the table whenever the eternal poker game goes in his disfavor. Those who pretended to see him as the little man baffled by the world's authority forgot the hidden cards, the knowledge that he will always win.

Robert Payne, *The Great God Pan*

Both clown and saint find themselves in conflict with a world that seems infinitely resourceful in its devices for crippling or murdering the self; as a minimum requirement, the clown withstands the reality, the saint transcends it, and in the most optimistic embodiments, they transform reality.

David D. Galloway

I am a sad, ragged little guy who is very serious about everything he attempts—no matter how futile or how foolish it appears to be. I am the hobo who found out the hard way that the deck is stacked, the dice "frozen," the race fixed and the wheel crooked, but there is always present that one, tiny, forlorn spark of hope still glimmering in his soul, which makes him keep trying.

Emmett Kelly with F. Beverly Kelley, *Clown*

The clown knows what it is to be the underdog, to be out of a job, to be done down by authority; but more than that, he knows he is not alone. In his magical and eccentric way, he triumphs through this self-knowledge. He transcends the buffeting, always gets up to live another day and shares his joy with us.

Beryl Hugill, *Bring on the Clowns*

He who has the courage to laugh is almost as much the master of the world as he who is ready to die.

Giacomo Leopardi

By the gods above,.is there anything that is better off than that class of men whom we generally call morons, fools, halfwits, and zanies—the most beautiful names I know of! ...they are not vexed by the thousand cares to which this life is subject. They do not feel shame or fear, they are not ambitious, they do not envy, they do not love....I wish you would think over for me, you wise fool, how by night and by day your soul is torn by so many carking cares; I wish you would gather into one heap all the discommodities of your life: then you will begin to understand from how many evils I have delivered my fools. Remember also that they are continually merry, they play, sing, and laugh; and what is more, they bring to others, wherever they may come, pleasure, jesting, sport, and laughter, as if they were created, by a merciful dispensation of the gods, for this one purpose—to drive away the sadness of human life.

Desiderius Erasmus, *The Praise of Folly*

Fools, they are the only nation worth men's envy or admiration; Free from care-or sorrow-taking, selves and others merry making.

Ben Jonson

...I have never—and I know many artistes—encountered that intolerable bore—the Clown with the Broken Heart.

Frank Foster, *Clowning Through*

Grimaldi...became depressed and ill and without telling his name sought the services of a well known doctor. "You need to laugh more and relax," the doctor told him. "I recommend you go regularly to the theatre and pay special attention to a comedian named Grimaldi."

Emmett Kelly with F. Beverly Kelley, *Clown*

Nothing, no experience good or bad, no belief, no cause, is in itself momentous enough to monopolize the whole of life to the exclusion of laughter.

Alfred North Whitehead

The clown's simplicity is one key to his special status. He simplifies the complicated. In a society that seeks elaborately contrived explanations for very basic emotional problems the clown is a throwback, a refreshing anachronism. One walk-around by a covey of sawdust comedians probably releases as much tension as weeks of therapy at the hands of a clinical psychologist, para or otherwise.

George Bishop, *The World of Clowns*

The mere possibility of employing laughter as a weapon
shows that it involves the idea of power.

Harald Höffding, Psykologiske Undersögelser

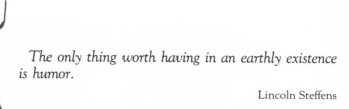

The only thing worth having in an earthly existence is humor.

Lincoln Steffens

I had rather a fool to make me merry than experience

Shakespeare, *As You Like It*

The rogue has freed us from shame. More than that, he has persuaded us that wasted affection, thwarted ambition, latent guilt are mere delusions to be laughed away. For how can we feel spiritual pain, if we are only animals?

Enid Welsford, *The Fool*

Nothing is sadder than laughter; nothing more beautiful, more magnificent, more uplifting and enriching than the terror of deep despair....That's why the intention of the...deepest and most honest writers of comedy is by no means only to amuse us, but wantonly to tear open our most painful scars so that we feel them all the more strongly.

Federico Fellini, *Fellini on Fellini*

Man is the only animal that laughs and weeps; for he is the only animal that is struck with the difference between what things are and what they might have been.

William Hazlitt

When we are born, we cry that we are come/ To this great stage of fools.

Shakespeare, *King Lear*

For the genius of the Fool is manifested by his power of deluding us into the belief that he can draw the sting of pain; by his power of surrounding us with an atmosphere of make-believe, in which nothing is serious, nothing is solid, nothing has abiding consequences. Under the dissolvent influence of his personality the iron network of physical, social and moral law, which enmeshes us from the cradle to the grave, seems—for the moment—negligible as a web of gossamer.

Enid Welsford, *The Fool*

And this power to make something out of nothing is given to all of us. All we need is the will to do it. To that eternal naive question reporters are for ever shouting at me: "Why did you become a clown?" I have only one reply. "Because I wanted to."

Grock (Adrien Wettach), *Life's a Lark*

[Emmett] Kelly's "Weary Willie" is a sad fellow—even more so than Chaplin's tramp—who never talks and never cracks a smile. His failure to accomplish simple tasks, much less to be as talented as the other circus performers, is cause for sympathetic laughter and not derision. He juggles three balls while balancing a peacock feather on his nose. When he drops a ball and bends over to look for it, the feather fails to fall from his nose. He is exposed as a phony, for everyone can see the feather is stuck in the clown's nose putty. An old piece of business, but with Kelly the point is his sad expression: he did the best he could.

John H. Towsen, *Clowns*

Agee on Keaton—No other comedian could do as much with the dead pan. He used this great, sad, motionless face to suggest various related things: a one-track mind near the track's end of pure insanity; mulish imperturbability under the wildest of circumstances; how dead a human being can get and still be alive; an awe-inspiring sort of patience and power to endure, proper to granite but uncanny in flesh and blood.

James Agee, *Agee on Film*

Human life is basically a comedy. Even its tragedies often seem comic to the spectator, and not infrequently they actually have comic touches to the victim. Happiness probably consists largely in the capacity to detect and relish them.

H.L. Mencken

Come, let us give a little time to folly...and even in a melancholy day let us find time for an hour of pleasure.

Oeuveres Francoises de Bona Venture

This I conceive to be the chemical function of humor: to change the character of our thought.

Lin Yutang

Invest in me my motley. Give me leave To speak my mind, and I will through and through Cleanse the foul body of the infected world, If they will patiently receive my medicine.

Shakespeare, *As You Like It*

In 1964, Norman Cousins, then editor of *Saturday Review*, fell critically ill with a degenerative disease of the spine. After doctors pronounced him incurable, he checked out of the hospital and into a hotel, armed with Vitamin C, reels of classic film comedy, and the works of James Thurber, Ogden Nash, S.J. Perelman, P.G. Wodehouse, and others, and cured himself with laughter. He found that ten minutes of belly laughter would give him two hours of pain-free sleep. After a session of laughter, Cousins' infection and inflammation rate fell by five points.

Based on a 1980 article in *Playboy* magazine

Live merrily as thou canst, for by honest mirth we cure many passions of the mind.

Robert Burton

Grock tells of entertaining maimed and crippled soldiers.
All my desire was to enable them to forget the terrible reality of their state... little by little [I] succeeded in conjuring up that deeply human and tragi-comic world of absurdity...nonsense...and at the same time profound wisdom. Blind eyes were raised, making the smile more eloquent...these young men...clapped their stumps together for lack of hands, stamped, shouted and laughed; laughed with all their hearts.

Grock (Adrien Wettach), *Grock: King of Clowns*

...that older and greater church to which I belong: the church where the oftener you laugh the better, because by laughter only can you destroy evil without malice....

George Bernard Shaw

As soon as you have made a thought, laugh at it.

Lao Tse

The secret source of humor is not joy but sorrow; there is no humor in heaven.

Mark Twain

It is the heart that is not sure of its God that is afraid to laugh in His presence.

F.D. Maurice

There is fun in heaven. God can play practical jokes upon Himself, draw chairs away from beneath His own posteriors, set His own turbans on fire, and steal His own petticoats when He bathes. By sacrificing good taste, this worship achieved what Christianity has shirked: the inclusion of merriment. All spirit as well as all matter must participate in salvation, and if practical jokes are banned, the circle is incomplete.

E.M. Forster, *A Passage to India*

People say: laughter is good for you. Oh, I agree. When a man's spent his life in the midst of laughter, then even when he's old his lungs are still full of oxygen.

Bario's speech from *The Clowns*
Federico Fellini, *Fellini on Fellini*

By their merry talk they cause sufferers to forget grief.

The Talmud

DUALITY:
FROM THE HARMONY OF
OPPOSITES COMES CREATION

The designation of the right and left hemispheres of the brain does not refer to a merely physical division, but to a more important psychic one. The right brain, popularly recognized as the center of creativity, is our inner Auguste, leaping about in unrestrainable motion. It is our intuition, so often distrusted but so rarely wrong: the weaver of our dreams and fantasies. This audacious Auguste is always being checked by the left brain, the reasoner and logician—our inner whiteface clown. The left brain acts the role of the authoritarian parent, the very correct adult who admonishes, "Don't be silly; when will you grow up?" But the left brain is also the planner, the organizer; and without its guidance the right brain could never channel its chaotic content into some recognizable and communicable form.

In the clown act, the two halves of the brain, like clown partners, work together in perfect synchronization to create an illusion of spontaneity within the constraints of tradition and discipline. The clown's right brain energies of intuition and playfulness are channeled by the left brain functions of rigorous training and careful planning. This inner equilibrium enables the professional clown to transmute the peculiar content of his individual mind into a collective artifact that expresses truths in a way that is accessible to a wider audience. Like any artist, the clown communicates a personal truth in such a way that it becomes a universal truth.

The clown embodies the most contradictory aspects of human nature. He boldly expresses the extremes of emotional behavior that exist potentially within each of us. Yet the clown is not a divided soul. On the contrary, his often frenetic uninhibitedness, his willingness to bare his emotions, bespeaks a wholeheartedness and freedom from inner conflict that we can only envy. In the clown, the divided energies—the contradictions and ambivalences—that sometimes paralyze us are reconciled. The clown, wearing his motley garb, waving his bladder, shaking his asses' ears, and crowing his cock's cry, tells us that humanity is broad enough to encompass all contradictions.

The clown is the child of duality, of paradox, of the eternally two-sided nature of man. He is at once wise and foolish, benign and cruel, holy and sinister, sexless and lecherous, spontaneous and calculating, comic and tragic. That he can comfortably embrace all these contradictions at once, and yet be so familiar and understandable to us, says something important about the human condition. And the tension that arises from our recognition of these contradictions generates the kind of knowing laughter that can only come from the most intimate and unspoken understanding.

A shallow and trivial exterior broken at intervals to reveal surprising depths is characteristic of the fool.

William Willeford, *The Fool and His Scepter*

Because the fool encompasses the opposite poles of energy, it is impossible to pin him down. The minute we think we have caught his essence, he slyly turns into his opposite and crows derisively from behind our backs.

Sallie Nichols, *Jung and Tarot*

Of all comedians [Charlie Chaplin] worked most deeply and most shrewdly within a realization of what a human being is, and is up against. The Tramp is as centrally representative of humanity, as many-sided and as mysterious, as Hamlet....

James Agee, *Agee on Film*

Disorder belongs to the totality of life, and the spirit of this disorder is the trickster. His function...is to add disorder to order and so make a whole, to render possible, within the fixed bounds of what is permitted, an experience of what is not permitted.

Paul V.A. Williams, *The Fool and the Trickster*

His many-sided nature is expressed by his bauble, a replica of his own head in cap and bells, with which he is often pictured in earnest conversation.

Sallie Nichols, *Jung and Tarot*

Clowns contain as many contradictions as humanity itself, and as performers they are always at great pains to make those contradictions felt. For to be a clown is to create and express a total personality. The title of an old play about an Elizabethan jester states it very simply: When You See Me You Know Me. *A great clown can communicate this comic personality sympathetically and instantaneously, whether he is alone in a spotlight on a stage, or trading gags, insults, and smacks of a slapstick with his fellow clowns, or simply as part of a vast comic landscape, filled with rocketing cars, flying pies, and other perils and pitfalls well known to circus buffs and fans of silent movie comedy.*

Lowell Swortzell, *Here Come the Clowns*

Fundamentally the clown depends not upon the external conflicts of hostile groups, but upon a certain inner contradiction in the soul of every man. In the first place we are creatures of the earth, propagating our species like other animals, in need of food, clothing, and shelter and of the money that procures them. Yet if we need money, are we so wholly creatures of the earth? If we need to cover our nakedness by material clothes or spiritual ideals, are we so like the other animals? This incongruity is exploited by the Fool.

Enid Welsford, *The Fool*

There have been many clown skits in which the clown's right hand literally does not know what his left is doing. This self-division is often expressed in the immediate physical appearance of the fool, for example, in costumes the right and left halves of which make a pattern of contrasts.

William Willeford, *The Fool and His Scepter*

As might be expected, the details of the Fool's costume combine many pairs of opposites within their design. His cap, although originally conceived as a satire on the monk's cowl, nevertheless betrays a serious connection with the spirit. Its bell, echoing the most solemn moment in the mass, calls man back to the childlike faith of fools, ringing out St. Paul's exhortation: "Let us be fools for Christ's sake."

Sallie Nichols, *Jung and Tarot*

The fool, through his actions, words, etc. convinces us of a qualitative difference between himself and us and thereby opens the way to a new relation between subject and object.

William Willeford, The Fool and His Scepter

The cause of laughter is simply the sudden perception of the incongruity between a concept and a real object.

Arthur Schopenhauer, The World as Will and Idea

...The clown is a creator, like the poet or the great tragic actor. He lives in his own world, and defies the world we know by virtue of his illuminations, his secret knowledge, his power to weave spells, his protean capacity to assume what forms he pleases. To him whatever is accidental in the world belongs to logic; whatever is logical and expected is to be regarded with disdain. The world is suspect; therefore he moves in his own world, in perpetual conflict with our world. He moves with the terrible directness of a child, seeing no obstacles to his progress, and like a child he falls over every obstacle in his path and cannot understand why he did not see them, or why there should be any conflict.

Robert Payne, The Great God Pan

A clown sees life simply, without complications. Something hurts—he cries. Something pleases him—he laughs. Something puzzles him—he frowns. Something frightens him—he runs. His exaggerated reactions are basic and straightforward.

George Bishop, The World of Clowns

Whether active or passive, fools are caught in problems of will. In his show the fool actor wants to be a fool, or he wants not to be a fool but cannot help being one; or else he is indifferent to his folly, in which case he contradicts what we think he should want to be. He usually does not want what we consciously want; if he does, he is usually not physically and mentally equipped to go about getting it as we would; if he is, he usually comes into conflict with the wills, nonfoolish and foolish, of other people and even apparently of things.

William Willeford, The Fool and His Scepter

I've got the sixth sense, but I don't have the other five.

Red Skelton

In many Tarot decks, the Fool is shown with a small dog which is nipping at him as if to communicate something...the Fool is in such close contact with his instinctual side that he does not need to look where he is going in the literal sense; his animal nature guides his steps.

Sallie Nichols, Jung and Tarot

When I say clown, I think of the Auguste. The two types of clown are in fact the white clown and the Auguste. The white clown stands for elegance, grace, harmony, intelligence, lucidity, which are posited in a moral way as ideal, unique, indisputable divinities. Then comes the negative aspect, because in this way the white clown becomes Mother and Father, Schoolmaster, Artist, the Beautiful, in other words what should be done. Then the Auguste, who would feel drawn to all these perfect attributes if only they were not so priggishly displayed, turns on them....This is the struggle between the proud cult of reason...and the freedom of instinct. The white clown and the Auguste are teacher and child, mother and small son, even the angel with the flaming sword and the sinner. In other words they are two psychological aspects of man: one which aims upwards, the other which aims downwards; two divided, separated instincts.

Federico Fellini, Fellini on Fellini

A man must have chaos within him to be able to give birth to a dancing star.

Friedrich Nietzsche

Perhaps the ultimate appeal of the clown lies in this double image; when they don the motley they become the agents of a great reversal of everything that is taken for granted in ordinary life. They may be tricked, beaten, or humiliated, but in their hands these things become matters for laughter and the sadness of life is transformed.

George Speaight, *The Book of Clowns*

One has often known many a wise word to come from a mouth reputed foolish; for that kind of madness, which uneducated and stupid people call folly, really may mean inspiration.

La Morosophie of Guillaume de la Pierre

Whimsical Walker (clown)—*I have never been able to define precisely what amuses an audience. I believe it is a question of inspiration.*

Ruth Manning-Sanders, *The British Circus*

The essence of all jokes, of all comedy, seems to be an honest or well-intentioned halfness; a non-performance of what is pretended to be performed, at the same time that one is giving loud pledges of performance.

R.W. Emerson, *The Comic*

To tell a good clown from a bad one is easy: either you are amused or you are not. But to distinguish a great clown from a good one is more difficult. A great clown will never give anyone the impression that he is playing a part. He never appears to have learnt his lines or studied his gestures. He seems to be a fathomless source of perfect improvisation. One is conscious of a power which appears limitless because it reverses our preconceived ideas....

Antony Hippisley Coxe, *A Seat at the Circus*

Nothing is impossible to your true artiste. This tremendous discipline of the will to which he subjects himself as a youngster, serves him in good stead now the years come thick upon him, so that he can still move mountains. We artistes view life from a point that is simplicity itself. It is the will that moves us, nothing less and nothing more. It is both our benefactor and our torment.

Grock (Adrien Wettach), *Life's a Lark*

Clowns are both unique and universal; the art of clowning involves at once spontaneous acts of creation, many years devoted to the expression of an individual comic identity, and many centuries of tradition, imitation, and unbroken cultural continuity.

Lowell Swortzell, *Here Come the Clowns*

Like the wire-walker, the clown treads a narrow path; he walks the knife-like edge which divides humor and pathos. He holds the balance between action and repose, between the clearest madness and the cloudiest sanity.

Antony Hippisley Coxe, *A Seat at the Circus*

As Dan Leno grew older, thin as a lamp-post with an uncanny gleam in his eyes, he became more boisterous and a little shriller. He played ping-pong with a frying pan and potatoes, or burlesqued a young girl at her harp lessons, and it was noticed that there was an added savagery and petulance in his performances. He expostulated, as always, with an irrational world, himself the only rational being in it, but the great grey London Times remarked that he was growing thoughtful and there was more than a touch of philosophical resignation in that remorseless stream of patter....The progress was probably inevitable: the thin line which separates the very comic from the tragic is thin as a hair, and in the end, Dan Leno went mad.

Robert Payne, *The Great God Pan*

Take the clowns, for example, those basically alien beings, funmakers, with little red hands, little thin-shod feet, red wigs under conical felt hats, their impossible lingo, their handstands, their stumbling and falling over everything, their mindless running to and fro and unserviceable attempts to help, their hideously unsuccessful efforts to imitate their serious colleagues—in tightrope-walking, for instance—which bring the crowd to a pitch of mad merriment. Are these ageless, half-grown sons of absurdity, at whom Stanko and I laughed so heartily (I, however, with a thoughtful fellow-feeling), are they human at all? With their chalk-white faces and utterly preposterous painted expressions—triangular eyebrows and deep perpendicular grooves in their cheeks under the reddened eyes, impossible noses, mouths twisted up at the corners into insane smiles—masks, that is, which stand in inconceivable contrast to the splendour of their costumes—black satin, for example, embroidered with silver butterflies, a child's dream—are they, I repeat, human beings, men that could conceivably find a place in everyday daily life? In my opinion it is pure sentimentality to say that they are "human too," with the sensibilities of human beings and perhaps even with wives and children. I honour them and defend them against ordinary bad taste when I say no, they are not, they are exceptions, side-splitting monsters of preposterousness, glittering, world-renouncing monks of unreason, cavorting hybrids, part human and part insane art.

Thomas Mann, *The Confessions of Felix Krull*

But what remains in the mind and in the spirit from the art of the Fratellini is first of all a beautiful flowing thing; a continuity of rhythm and vitality that creates sheerly through the eyes, a separable existence of its own. The own. The source of their art's perfection lies in a purity, a freedom from everything outside itself and its own moment. Life springs in their art from a certain mysterious, careless exactitude. I watch them and derive from their performance something like the ideality of music....But the art of this clowning differs from music in that...[this ideality is] not left pure and general and abstract but... [is] brought into collision with downright everyday facts....In this art...we have the de-defeated, resounding, incongruous human soul, comical and endearing.

S. Young,
"The Fratellini,"
New Republic,
July 23, 1924

41

LINKAGE: OURSELVES AND THE FOOL

Probably any sensitive observer who has watched a clown perform has felt a vague sense of uneasiness and even embarrassment in the presence of the intense emotions the clown expresses. For the clown exposes the nakedest human emotions, presenting them with the unabashed honesty of a child or primitive. Embarrassed reactions to other people's emotional excesses are an almost universal phenomenon, and even clowns, being human themselves, share it. The Italian clowns I have known admitted occasional embarrassment over the reactions of some of the people they have performed for, though they were fully aware that it is part of the clown's function to evoke some sense of disquiet and uneasiness in his audience.

The clown, creating out of the matter of his own soul, gains momentum from the reactions of his audience. This symbiotic relationship between the clown and his audience exists on several levels. When we laugh at the clown's antics and ordeals, we are responding to the central truth of the clown act: that the figure on the stage, on the screen, or in the circus ring is not an individual but an expression of ourselves; that his antics are reenactments of our follies. We may consciously identify with the underdog Auguste in the clown act, and cheer to see the foolish but good-hearted innocent triumph over the pompous whiteface bully, but surely there is a part of us that recognizes the elements of both innocent and bully in our own behavior. And when we smirk at the clown's blunders, or laugh at his caricatures of character types we find offensive or ludicrous, some part of us must be aware that we too are fair targets for mockery.

The clown act cannot exist in a vacuum. It has no meaning without an audience, without someone to behold it and participate in it through the laughter of recognition. The audience's laughter is the expression of its understanding, the essential link in the chain that makes the communication of the clown act complete. When the audience reacts to and moves with the clown, and the clown matches himself to his audience, the dynamics of the act are truly realized. In the midst of laughter, when the boundary between clown and audience suddenly blurs and fades, there is a magical moment of shared creation.

Clowns are ordinary folk, jest like you and me, only worse.

Edward Fitchner, Circus Tales

Without laughter life on our planet would be intolerable. So important is laughter to us that humanity highly rewards members of one of the most unusual professions on earth, those who make a living by inducing laughter in others. This is very strange if you stop to think of it: that otherwise sane and responsible citizens should devote their professional energies to causing others to make sharp, explosive barking-like exhaltations.

Steve Allen, Funny People

You would hardly appreciate the comic if you felt yourself isolated from others. Laughter appears to stand in need of an echo.

Henri Bergson, Laughter

A good clown caricatures his fellow men; a great one parodies himself.

Pierre Mariel

A great clown will not stoop to caricature. We caricature only those things we despise. To ridicule the things we love demands the higher art of parody. Just as the Greeks would parody a sacred drama immediately following its first performance, so the clown in the modern circus will parody the things we hold most sacred today. To do this he must be a great clown.

Antony Hippisley Coxe, A Seat at the Circus

The freedom to indulge in parody and unexpected truthtelling, and the additional freedom to be wantonly licentious without incurring blame are the two privileges of the fool which make it worth the while of normal men occasionally to assume his role.

Barbara Swain, Fools and Folly

The maintenance of jesters at court and in the households of titled families began in ancient times and continued until the seventeenth century. This practice dramatizes the idea that we must make room for the renegade factor in ourselves and admit him to our inner court....Accepted in our inner council, the Fool can offer us fresh ideas and new energy....Without the Fool's blunt observations and wise epigrams, our inner landscape might become a sterile wasteland.

Sallie Nichols, Jung and Tarot

Unfortunately, like Henry VIII, Elizabeth I, and many other authorities throughout the ages, we tend not only to ignore this part of ourselves, the intuitive creative unconscious, but worse, we disparage and debase it, and often repress it altogether.

Under Henry VIII the position of the court jester was abolished when the church stepped in to declaim against their way of life, and in the reign of Queen Elizabeth I they were actually persecuted ...being classified in company with Ruffians, Blasphemers, Thieves, Vagabonds.

P.M Morris, Chipperfield's Circus

How lecherous, scurrilous and worthless are these swollen bladders; what noise as if of farting and as loathsome.

Le Romans de Valhubert, Lyons 1593

The victimised clown is the scapegoat of man; the herdlike fury of the mob can be heaped upon his shoulders and impossible cruelties inflicted upon a deformed victim whose life represents a comic nightmare. Genius and madness, love and hate, tolerance and persecution, beauty and the beast, the clown is man's alter-ego.

Rupert Croft-Cooke and Peter Cotes, *Circus*

Charlie Chaplin enjoyed unparalleled fame and popularity while at the same time he was the subject of unlimited hostility from religious/moral groups, the press, big business and the U.S. government. The same man, much loved and hated, was both a public idol and a public affront. But he went his own way, in spite of it all.

...I am not at all the kind of man who wants to make merry only in the circus, and for the rest of his time goes about like any ordinary citizen, solid and self-contained. My attitude has always been that if I am a clown in the ring I can and should be a clown out of the ring. Either you should be a thing or not be it.

Grock (Adrien Wettach), *Life's a Lark*

Frank "Slivers" Oakley, the immortal baseball clown, used to tell about a performance in Chicago that illustrates how little dignity a clown has. Slivers was waiting on the ramp to go on, when a little boy threw a tin can at him and hit him in the eye. Blood spurted and his face and costume were quickly covered. As Slivers strove to staunch the flow he swears he heard the boy yell, "Hey Pop, see me hit that clown in the eye?" "Yes, Son." "It was a peach of a shot, wasn't it, Pa?" "It was, my son."
Slivers used to say, "The clown isn't really thought of as a human being. He's an indestructible form of life somewhere between a grasshopper and an orangutan."

A.E. Hotchner, *The Greatest Club on Earth*

But if the fool is "he who gets slapped," the most successful fool is "he who is none the worse for his slapping," and this introduces a new and interesting factor into the comic situation. The fool is now no longer a mere safety valve for the suppressed instincts of the bully, he provides a subtler balm for the fears and wounds of those afflicted with the inferiority complex, the greater part of humanity if we may believe our psychologists. It is all very well to laugh at the buffeted simpleton; we too are subject to the blows of fate, and of people stronger and wiser than ourselves, in fact we are the silly Clown, the helpless Fool.

Enid Welsford, *The Fool*

The clown's ability to evoke feelings of superiority in the spectator plays a hidden role in all clowning.

John H. Towsen, *Clowns*

Perhaps we might say [The Fool] represents a redemptive factor within ourselves that urges us on towards individuation. He is that part of us which, innocently yet somehow quite knowingly, finds itself embarked upon the quest for self-knowledge. Through him, we fall into seemingly foolish experiences which we later recognize as crucial to the pattern of our lives....From the stroke of The Fool one never recovers. And who would want to!

Sallie Nichols, *Jung and Tarot*

A good clown catches his audience in a spell, a spell of laughter and awareness. They are his and he can do anything with them. It is truly magic.

Edward Fitchner, *Circus Tales*

A gay companion is as a wagon to him that is wearied by the way.

Robert Burton

Only those jokes which are directly related to the primary emotions remain constantly popular. Clownship, therefore, is to be distinguished by its upholding of the fundamentals of laughter, by its regard for the elemental jokes as if they were the rites of a religion....

M. Willson Disher, *Clowns and Pantomimes*

An understanding of human nature is not born in a day; it comes of experience, and it comes of wide and varied contacts. In order to make humanity laugh at a picture of its own folly...one must know that folly. And not only must one know it, but one must sympathize with it and forgive it—or how should folly laugh without bitterness at its own image?

Ruth Manning-Sanders, *The English Circus*

The clown is not particularly interested in making people comfortable; tragi-comedy is his real specialty—sharing all his emotions with an audience in a way that often seems childlike and naive but is really something of an artistic mystery.

Lowell Swortzell, *Here Come the Clowns*

No sooner do I get upon the stage than all my self-protective armour peels away from me and I am a recording instrument as sensitive as a mimosa plant. There is nothing I cannot feel and nothing I do not react to.

Grock (Adrien Wettach), *Life's a Lark*

...the clown must be ever on the alert: audiences differ; some are easy, some are difficult, some heavy, some forthcoming, some slow, some bright, some dull. As soon as he enters the ring, the clown, with the skill of a psychologist, but with the speed of intuition, must know how his audience will react. He may seem to be doing the same old funny stuff day after day; but, depend upon it, if he can draw the same happy tears of laughter from country audiences and town audiences, from English and French audiences, as all really great clowns can, the funny stuff is not precisely the same—it has its subtle variations.

Ruth Manning-Sanders, *The English Circus*

"If you find yourself able to make people laugh," Otto Griebling believed, *"it is God's gift. You have to do everything from the bottom of your heart. I don't go in for slapstick. I let the emotion come from inside and penetrate the eyes. I'm the same man underneath, I'm always part of the human tragicomedy."*

John H. Towsen, *Clowns*

By laughing at me, they [the audience] really laugh at themselves, and realizing that they have done this gives them a sort of spiritual second wind for going back into the battle [of life].

Emmett Kelly with F. Beverly Kelley, *Clown*

The clown...cannot do well if the audience is not with him, for their response is the meaning of his act. It is a two-partner business; and the one partner is helpless if the other partner fails him. For this reason, clowns have been known to take their lives in the complete spiritual bankruptcy of finding themselves out of touch with their audience.

Ruth Manning-Sanders, *The English Circus*

Although clowns generally live to what is cheerfully known as a "ripe old age," in spite of the hazards of their profession, there have been a few notable exceptions. Grimaldi, through overwork, injury, and a heartbreaking personal life, died at age fifty-eight. But perhaps saddest of all are those who lose contact with their audience—for whatever reason. Marceline, the great French clown who was Chaplin's master, died

...in a lonely lodging-room with a pawn ticket and six dollars in his pockets and a bullet sent through his brain by his own hand.

Literary Digest, December 1937

It wasn't old age. He was only fifty-four. He was as lively as ever when he tried to make his "comebacks." But they didn't laugh at him as they used to.... So he played the final act all alone, on his knees, in a lodging-house room.

New York Evening World, November 1937

I have known many clowns, but never have I met a gloomy one. Steady, yes, and perhaps on the whole, quiet, with that serene quietness which so often goes with a merry heart. If I were asked to name two of the clown's most outstanding characteristics, I should say kindness and humanity, and these two qualities do not live with gloom.

Ruth Manning-Sanders, *The English Circus*

[Johnny Patterson, the Irish Clown]...the greatest singing artist of the time died in 1889 under the circus tent, having refused to go to a hospital. So strong was the animus of the church against circus people at that period, no minister could be found who was willing to preach poor Patterson's funeral sermon, and no cemetery would receive his body.

In order to give him a decent burial, we all chipped in and bought a piece of ground, in which all that was mortal of one of the best buffoons that ever donned motley was laid to rest, just as dawn was breaking. Pete Conklin, the clown, read the Episcopal service for the dead, which I'm sure would not have pleased Johnny as he was a county Donegal man of Roman Catholic faith. So passed, under the rays of the rising sun, a man who made millions laugh and whose rollicking rhymes were enjoyed by men, women, and children of three continents.

Robert Sherwood, *Here We Are Again*

The clown is a mirror in which man sees himself in a grotesque, deformed, ridiculous image. He is man's shadow. As so he will be forever. It is as if we were to ask ourselves: "Is death the shadow? Does the shadow die?" For the shadow to die, the sun must be directly above our heads; then the shadow vanishes. The completely enlightened man has made his grotesque, ridiculous, deformed aspects disappear. Faced with so well-finished a creature, the clown—seen as his crippled aspect—would have no reason to exist. But the clown will not vanish, that's for sure. He will be merely assimilated. In other words, the irrational, the childish and the instinctive will no longer be seen with an eye that deforms them, that makes them deformed.

Federico Fellini, *Fellini on Fellini*

He deserves Paradise who makes his companions laugh.

The Koran

THE PRESENT
AND FUTURE CLOWN

The great comics of the silent film era—Charlie Chaplin, Buster Keaton, Harold Lloyd—gave new life to the perennial figure of the bewildered innocent, constantly at odds with a progressively mechanized, de-humanized society. How prophetic they were! Now that vast bureaucracies are further governing our lives, and our frustrations are growing in the face of increasing confusion and ambiguity, we need the clown more than ever. And yet, in an age when the substance and quality of our entertainment is determined by computerized ratings systems and the homogenizing effects of mass media, the future of the professional clown often seems uncertain at best. Many believe that the golden age of the clown has already long since passed. Gone, they lament, are the Grocks and the Grimaldis, the Fratellinis and the Deburaus—replaced now by painted and costumed posturers who are suited to do little more than decorate county fairs or preside over the grand openings of fast food restaurants. To those who fear that the clown is a faded anachronism, his modern incarnations seem to be mere shadows—albeit still colorful ones—of his former glory.

Where are the great clowns now? Perhaps they have never really left us. If we stubbornly insist on believing that the great clowns belong to the past only, to the fading realm of the theatre and the circus, then we are bound to look with some disdain on the film comics, stand-up comedians, and television comedy characters who have arisen to take the traditional clown's place. But perhaps our disappointment with the modern clown has less to do with his shortcomings than with our own restrictive notions of what a clown ought to be. For the clown has always been more than a zinc-white face and colored greasepaint features, more than a baggy costume and a trunkful of props and gags. In his traditional guises the clown is the living embodiment of a past that somehow seems far removed from our own time. But he is also a highly adaptable creature, the variety of his forms increasing as his metier changes and expands throughout the ages. The clown can be whatever he wishes to be, change hats as often as he pleases, but his essence remains the same.

The clown of today, reflecting perhaps the new social freedoms, is once more a wanderer, no longer bound to the restrictions of the circus or the conventions of costume and make-up. Street theatre clowns brighten our grey city-scapes with an irreverent socio-political humor that would be impossible to present in the family-oriented circus setting. Small comedy stores where aspiring young comedians vie energetically for the audience's laughter are becoming fixtures in many major cities. And the painted face of the more traditional clown is appearing in a broader range of settings than ever before: in the parks and the community centers, in children's hospitals and on university campuses, at carnivals and festive public events. He is once more among the people, still an entertainer but no longer relegated to a narrow sphere of activity. It is hardly likely, though, that he will ever entirely sever his ties to the circus—his most recognizable home for the past two hundred years.

For now, the clown's most lucrative domains are television and film, and he will continue to take advantage of the potential of these media until even better showcases for his talent come along. With more people than ever before—some of them with established careers—applying to clown schools and enrolling in clownology courses, we need not fear the demise of the traditional clown in our society. It is unlikely, indeed, that the clown could die out in any culture. We need the clown, need him in his roles as scapegoat and sage, critic and counselor. And for as long as we exist, he will be with us to mock us and prod us, to laugh at us and hold up the mirror to our foibles: to celebrate, with great irreverence, the human condition.

"Dear Lady Emily," says Miss Allscrip....."Dear Lady Emily, don't you dote upon folly?"
"To Ecstasy!" replied her ladyship. "I only despair of seeing it well kept up."

from *The Heiress*—quoted in Barbara Swain, *Fools and Folly*

Traditional folly always thrived in times and situations of transition. In many different traditional societies people have ceremonially reversed the existing order of things during periods of time in which fundamental changes took place. The ancient Roman Saturnalia, the medieval Feast of Fools, and the contemporary European carnival are examples of such foolish transition ceremonies. During the transition from the old to the new year, during Shrove Tide or Lent—a period in which nature regenerates and in which the Easter drama of death and resurrection is commemorated—during marriage and funeral ceremonies, during initiation rites, people throughout the ages and in culturally quite different contexts have staged foolish performances, changed sex roles, reversed social hierarchies, overthrown value patterns, violated tabooed norms, and acted generally as in a mirror fashion.

Anton C. Zijderveld, *Reality in a Looking-Glass*

To what are we to attribute the decay of the circus? One of the reasons... was the wave of gentility that passed over the middle classes... towards the end of the nineteenth century, a movement which swept away the old music hall...[and] the old Harlequinade, with its red hot poker and sausages....

Barnum [then] killed the circus by developing its least attractive elements. The circus under his influence became a monstrous...loud, distracting and bewildering display....

The circus, to succeed, must bring all eyes and minds to focus, and this above all is the true function of a clown.

J. Palmer, "The Fratellini,"
Fortnightly Review, January 1926

It is the clown who can make or break a circus by the tricks he does, his presence, personality, his gaiety in the ring and the mystique of his sadness out of it.

Rupert Croft-Cooke and Peter Cotes, *Circus*

Barnum said, "clowns and elephants were the pegs on which a circus hung." Perhaps the elephants could be dispensed with, but a circus without clowns—unthinkable.

Frank Foster, *Pink Coat, Spangles, and Sawdust*

The modern clown... does not have quite the same standing in show business as he had years ago. There was a time when most clowns could ride, do the ring or bars, work the trapeze, juggle or present horses in an emergency. Now few of them can do more than their entrees, gags and run-ins, with the result that many proprietors begin to look on the clowns as something like the measles that you can't help having around.

Butch Reynolds, *Broken Hearted Clown*

To me it is a pathetic sight when an act finishes... and [in] comes a horde of miscellaneous clowns to keep the ring busy until... they are summarily called off.

M. Gorham, *Showmen and Suckers*

...it is useless to pretend that all is well with circus clowning today. In England, and Europe generally, there are a handful of good clowns, but in many large circuses they rely too much on mechanical tricks, and in some small circuses the clowns simply keep the audience occupied while the props are set up for the next act....Clowns are often the worst paid members of circus companies, and it is a vicious circle with poor clowns earning low pay which discourages ambitious artistes from becoming circus clowns.

George Speaight, *The Book of Clowns*

In 1972... Carson and Barnes Circus toured successfully without the "pegs" [clowns] for seven straight months....No irate customers wanted their money back.

David Lewis Hammarstrom, *Behind the Big Top*

The great difference between the old-time circuses and those of today is the status of the clown. In other days he was the principal attraction, the success of the shown often depending on his efforts. He improvised, told stories, argued with the ringmaster, commented on the acts and sang songs. Now the clown is usually one of a dozen who fill up the gap between one act and another, and whose chief stock-in-trade are bizarre costumes, knock-about business and acrobatics.

Rupert Croft-Cooke, *The Circus Book*

Nowadays it is on the small family and tenting shows that we have to look for our clowns at their best. Barnum said that clowns and elephants were the pegs upon which a circus hung; but, in the big modern shows, as far as the clowns are concerned, this is no longer true. It is sad to see so much talent, and, in many cases, actual genius, wasted in those brief ambles round the ring whilst the ring-boys are hurrying to clear away the properties of one act and bring in the properties for the next.

Ruth Manning-Sanders, *The English Circus*

The clown of the circus is not secure from the fate that has overcome his brother of the stage. Just as the over-elaboration of the pantomime destroyed the Grimaldi tradition so the vogue, instituted by Phineas Barnum, of the mammoth circus, threatens to oust this primitive fun from the ring.

M. Willson Disher, *Clowns and Pantomimes*

The Fool is a wanderer: energetic, ubiquitous and immortal.

Sallie Nichols, Jung and Tarot: An Archetypal Journey

Charlie Cairoli, who, after sixty-five years as an auguste, was in a position to know, believed that the traditional clown would die out altogether if he did not change to suit the tenor of the times....He based his entrees upon everyday topical situations, for he believed that much of the laughter he got was from people seeing a situation in which they could imagine themselves. Change was important, he insisted. A clown must add something different to his act all the time; people would laugh at it if it had a basis in reality.

Beryl Hugill, *Bring on the Clowns*

It is perhaps no surprise that the audience for sadistic humor has enlarged given the underlying, and quite disturbing, fact that there is far more evidence of cruelty in our society than there was a quarter-century ago.

Steve Allen, *Funny People*

[Jung] proved empirically that consciousness is not just a rational process and that modern man precisely is sick and deprived of meaning because for centuries now...he has pursued a slanted development on the assumption that consciousness and the powers of reason are one and the same thing.

Sallie Nichols, *Jung and Tarot*

It is not quite clear that the change of mental climate which was so fatal to the fool is proving in the long run altogether wholesome to ourselves. Something has been lost. We feel drawn to the fool as he weeps in the emptiness of Versailles. Scientific enlightenment is good, yet it would also be good to regain the sense of glory, which does somehow seem to be connected with humility, and the acceptance of limitation.

Enid Welsford, *The Fool*

In Russia, circus clowning seems to be at a higher level than elsewhere in the world. It may be that the more natural, less grotesque, style of playing adopted by Russian clowns in recent years will spread to circuses elsewhere. It does not make them any less funny. The cause of clowning in the Soviet Union is not helped by the Party officials who declare that clowns must play their part in the national struggle, ridicule western fashions, and generally advance the Marxist-Leninist education of the people. But there is a germ of truth in the idea that clowning, if it is to be a living force, should spring from contemporary life. There is a real danger that clowning in the West may become fossilized in a highly stylized and no longer funny tradition of character and costume.

George Speaight, *The Book of Clowns*

If you ask me what I think...well, I can't really say. Because I've known so many clowns, and nearly all of them made people laugh; but it's all been such a long time, and in these last few years I'm not sure that the audiences laugh the way they used to, any more. I used to make them laugh a lot myself, with my brother Dario, and Rhum, and my sons Nello and Freddy...we had an act with a cake inside a hat—oh, that was very, very funny! Everyone roared with laughter when we came into the ring....No, I don't think it's all over and done with.

Bario's speech from *The Clowns*
Federico Fellini, *Fellini on Fellini*

For several years now the clown has taken on a great importance; not in the sense of the traditional circus, which is dead, but as a part of the search for what is laughable and ridiculous in man....We put the emphasis on the rediscovery of our own individual clown—the one that has grown up within us and which society does not allow us to express.

Jacque Lecoq, *Yale Theatre*, 4, no. 1 (Winter 1973)

There may be something in the argument that clowning is essentially anarchic and disruptive of society, and to turn it into a didactic medium...is to emasculate it and rob it of its true character. Clowns cannot become mouthpieces of Big Brother and remain true to their calling.

George Speaight, *The Book of Clowns*

I perform the best of all possible tasks, for I spread mirth and merriment around me wherever I go and no one is gladder than I to be able to do it.

Grock (Adrien Wettach), *Life's a Lark*

...the Charlie who appears in Modern Times...has one good look at industry and flees in terror. Life in a dog-kennel, he suggests, is infinitely superior to life in a cogwheel. Once again comedy has become the decoration for desperate truths, for the agony of our time is precisely that we are caught up in the wheels of machines which have never known where they are going and never will know. Slowly, ineluctably, the machine is beginning to master us. As so often in Chaplin's films, the comedy is pure terror; and when Charlie is caught in the wheels and sent spinning from one cog to another and is fed with an automatic feeder which is insanely out of temper, so that it feeds him with nuts and bolts with the same careless effrontery as it flings pies at his face, we are aware that the monstrous invention is hardly more than a slight exaggeration. We laugh not because of Charlie's predicament, but because we are suddenly confronted with the world's predicament, and surely there is a touch of hysteria in our laughter.

Robert Payne, *The Great God Pan*

He was born with the gift of laughter and a sense that the world was mad.

Rafael Sabatini

The King, the Priest, and the Fool all belong to the same regime, all belong essentially to a society shaped by belief in Divine order, human inadequacy, efficacious ritual; and there is no real place for any of them in a world increasingly dominated by the notions of the puritan, the scientist, and the captain of industry; for strange as it may seem the fool in cap and bells can only flourish among a people who have sacraments, who value symbols as well as tools, and cannot forever survive the decay of faith in divinely imposed authority, the rejection of all taboo and mysterious inspiration.

Enid Welsford, *The Fool*

There is a hunger among young men and women today to express themselves through the medium of clowning. Perhaps they seek some escape into a world of fantasy from a too rigid and materialist civilization; or perhaps they sense an abysmal catastrophe hanging over our society and can find no other response but to laugh at it. Whatever the reason, more people are trying to be clowns today than ever before in history.

George Speaight, *The Book of Clowns*

The public has a rooted idea that all you have to do in order to become a clown is to practice a whole week long every morning in front of the glass, rolling your eyes and putting out your tongue as far as it will go. A tongue and a looking glass are certainly part of a clown's outfit, and by no means to be despised, either of them, but a long tongue and a big mouth no more go to complete a clown than a paint brush does an artist or horn-rimmed spectacles a poet. No clown can be a real clown without the help of tradition and method, and an exhaustive technical training for his profession.

Grock (Adrien Wettach), *Life's a Lark*

There is nothing essentially immoral or blasphemous or rebellious about clownage. On the contrary it may easily act as a social preservative by providing a corrective to the pretentious vanity of officialdom, a safety-valve for unruliness, a wholesome nourishment to the sense of secret spiritual independence of that which would otherwise be the intolerable tyranny of circumstance.

Enid Welsford, *The Fool*

...the state ought to consider opening a school for clowns. No age limit: when a man's got the vocation for it, he can dedicate himself to it even at forty, and become a clown. Take an engineer, say. Now if he has the vocation for it, he can become a clown. University graduates, doctors, lawyers. They've all been excellent....It's good for your health to be a clown, you know. It's good because you can do anything you like: break everything, tear everything, set fire to things, roll on the floor, and nobody ticks you off, nobody stops you. The children wish they could do whatever they liked: tear things, set fire to things, roll on the floor...and so they love you. We ought to support them, and encourage them to go ahead with a good school for clowns, open to children—particularly to children. That way they could do what they liked, enjoy themselves and give enjoyment to others. It's a good job, and if you can do it you earn just as much as you would in an office. Why do parents want their children to work in offices and not be clowns? It's all wrong.

Bario's speech from *The Clowns*
Federico Fellini, *Fellini on Fellini*

...it is after all the clown who performs the most impossible feats in the circus ring. Simply by daring to exist the clown shows more daring than any trapeze artist. He is the immortal who comes to us out of death, bearing a burden of ghostly memories, the possessor of a mechanical neon-lit heart and a nose on which the graveyard earth still clings. He is all we have left in the modern world of the deathless delight-makers, and as he seeks to turn our attention from the bare legs of the girls and the silken horses, he is merely insisting on his right to proclaim his own immortality.

Robert Payne, *The Great God Pan*

SELECTED BIBLIOGRAPHY

Allen, Steve. *Funny People*. New York: Stein and Day, 1981.

Ballantine, Bill. *Clown Alley*. Boston: Little, Brown, 1982.

Bishop, George. *The World of Clowns*. Los Angeles: Brooke House, 1976.

Coxe, Antony Hippisley. *A Seat at the Circus*. Rev. ed. Hamden, Connecticut: Archon Books, 1980.

Croft-Cooke, Rupert, ed. *The Circus Book*. London: Sampson Low, Marston and Co., Ltd., n.d.

Croft-Cooke, Rupert, and Cotes, Peter. *Circus: A World History*. New York: Macmillan Publishing Co., Inc., 1976.

Disher, M. Willson. *Clowns and Pantomimes*. 1925. Reprint. New York and London: Benjamin Blom, 1968.

Erasmus, Desiderius. *The Praise of Folly*. Translated by Hoyt Hopewell Hudson. Princeton: Princeton University Press, 1941.

Fellini, Federico. *Fellini on Fellini*. Translated by Isabel Quigley. New York: Delacorte Press/Seymour Lawrence, 1976.

Findlater, Richard [Kenneth Bain]. *Joe Grimaldi: His Life and Theatre*. 2d ed. Cambridge and New York: Cambridge University Press, 1978. Originally published in 1955 under the title, *Grimaldi, King of Clowns*.

Grock [Adrien Wettach]. *Grock: King of Clowns.* London: Methuen, 1957.

-----. *Life's a Lark.* Translated by Madge Pemberton. 1931. Reprint. New York and London: Benjamin Blom, 1969.

Hammarstrom, David Lewis. *Behind the Big Top.* South Brunswick and New York: A.S. Barnes and Co., Inc., 1980.

Harzberg, Hiler, and Moss, Arthur. *Slapstick and Dumbbell—A Casual Survey of Clowns and Clowning.* New York: J. Lawren, 1924.

Hugill, Beryl. *Bring on the Clowns.* New Jersey: Chartwell Books, Inc., 1980.

Kelly, Emmett. *Clown.* With F. Beverly Kelley. New York: Prentice Hall, Inc., 1954.

Manning-Sanders, Ruth. *The English Circus.* London: Werner Laurie, 1952.

Nichols, Sallie. *Jung and Tarot: An Archetypal Journey.* Introd. by Laurens van der Post. New York: Samuel Weiser, 1980.

Niklaus, Thelma. *Harlequin, or The Rise and Fall of a Bergamask Rogue.* New York: George Braziller, Inc., 1956.

Payne, Robert. *The Great God Pan.* New York: Hermitage House, 1952.

Pearce, Richard. *Stages of the Clown: Perspectives on Modern Fiction from Dostoyevsky to Beckett.* Preface by Harry T. Moore. Illinois: Southern Illinois University Press, 1970.

Sherwood, Robert. *Here We Are Again: Recollections of an Old Circus Clown.* Indianapolis: Bobbs-Merrill Co., 1926.

Speaight, George. *The Book of Clowns*. New York: Macmillan Publishing Co., Inc., 1980.

Swain, Barbara. *Fools and Folly: During the Middle Ages and the Renaissance*. New York: Columbia University Press, 1932.

Swortzell, Lowell. *Here Come the Clowns*. New York: The Viking Press, 1978.

Sypher, Wylie, ed. *Comedy: An Essay on Comedy by George Meredith. "Laughter" by Henri Bergson*. New York: Doubleday and Co., Inc., 1956.

Taylor, Robert Lewis. *Center Ring: The People of the Circus*. New York: Doubleday and Co., Inc., 1956.

Tietze-Conrat, Erica. *Dwarfs and Jesters in Art*. New York: Phaidon, 1957.

Towsen, John H. *Clowns*. New York: Hawthorn Books, Inc., 1976.

Verney, Peter. *Here Comes the Circus*. New York and London: Paddington Press, 1978.

Welsford, Enid. *The Fool: His Social and Literary History*. London: Faber and Faber Ltd., 1935.

Williams, Paul V.A., ed. *The Fool and the Trickster: Studies in Honour of Enid Welsford*. Great Britain: D.S. Brewer, Ltd.; New Jersey: Rowman and Littlefield, 1979.

Willeford, William. *The Fool and His Scepter: A Study in Clowns and Jesters and Their Audience*. Illinois: Northwestern University Press, 1969.

Wykes, Alan. *Circus! An Investigation into What Makes the Sawdust Fly*. London: Jupiter Books, Ltd., 1977.

Zijderveld, Anton C. *Reality in a Looking-Glass: Rationality Through an Analysis of Traditional Folly*. London: Routledge and Kegan Paul, 1982.

This book was set in Goudy Old Style by Typecast Graphics of San Diego
The color separations were made by Photolitho AG, Gossau—Zurich, Switzerland
Designed by Paul Cline and Sandra Darling
Printed at The Green Tiger Press, Inc., San Diego, California
Bound by Lonnie's Trade Bindery, Lemon Grove, California